# The Book of Life

ELIZABETH BECKETT

Copyright © 2015 by the author. All rights reserved. No part of this book may be photocopied or otherwise reproduced without written permission from the author.

Contact author at:
www.elizabethbeckettbooks.com

ISBN 13: 978-1512221169
ISBN-10: 1512221163

Cover design: Authoright
Interior design: The Publishing Pro, LLC,
Colorado Springs, Colorado

# Dedication

To Afram, and the others.

# Contents

|  | Prologue | 1 |
|---|---|---|
| 1. | Eyes of Kohl | 3 |
| 2. | The Pyramid and the Energy Spiral | 12 |
| 3. | The Ladder of Lessons and the Djed-Column | 21 |
| 4. | The Sacred Elementals and the Alchemy of Spirit | 39 |
| 5. | Hieroglyphs and the Alphabet | 44 |
| 6. | Temples of the Skies | 49 |
| 7. | Our Colorful Universe | 57 |
| 8. | Sacred Sounds and the Seven Rays | 71 |
| 9. | Trans-Meditation | 85 |
| 10. | Judgement and Universal Laws | 108 |
| 11. | Representations of Initiations Passed | 115 |
| 12. | Egypt and Egyptian Gods | 138 |
| 13. | Attaining Illumination | 153 |
| 14. | High-Alphabet Glyphs | 163 |
| 15. | Ovocula of the High-Alphabet | 181 |
| 16. | Glyph Combinations and Animation Symbols | 200 |
|  | Epilogue | 214 |
|  | Glossary of Terms | 217 |

# Prologue

Welcome to the Pharonic Mystical Schools—also known as the Mysterie Schools of ancient Egypt.

We are a sect of ascended priests and priestesses, or pharaohs, from the schools; we would like to take you back to that time, so that you might remember what we taught. The schools are long-destroyed, but the teachings are eternal. Most of the concepts of our Mysterie Schools are still valid, but some have evolved over time. Either way, in some form or another, they all resonate with absolute, divine truth.

The existence of our schools spanned many thousands of years in Egypt—almost 10,000 Earth years. The teachings were brought to Egypt from the lost continent of Atlantis and later from the Hathors—a spiritually advanced intergalactic civilization.

Many school systems have been similar to the Egyptian Mysterie Schools on Earth. These existed at different times on different continents, but the teachings are alike. We are graduates from the Egyptian (or Pharonic) Mystical Schools specifically and so will focus on that knowledge. You might prefer the Greek, British, Asian, Aztec, or one of the other school systems—and we understand that.

We are very pleased to bring you some of the teachings of our

Mysterie Schools, or the Book of Life, in all its colorful vibrancy and mystical beauty. Although it is not our intention to take you down a spiritual path within the confines of this book, we describe some objective concepts of an initiate's passage through the School of Life, and hope to rectify some misconceptions.

# 1
## Eyes of Kohl

The translation for our school system is usually given as Mysterie Schools, but we understand them more accurately as Mystical Schools. The difference is subtle but important. The word *mysterie* suggests that there is some hidden knowledge that the soul can never attain—something that remains god-like and ever-separate from the seeker. The term *mystical* refers more aptly to the attainment of a direct connection to the god-essence of the self; in other words, reaching divinity through surrender of the ego and stripping away falsities that are not part of the soul's true path. The will of the soul is the selfsame will of god, since each soul is a piece of the synergy that is the god-energy. In reaching illumination, the seeker realizes that there is no mystery other than that which they hide from themselves. Therefore, we prefer *Mystical Schools*, but we will use *Mysterie Schools* interchangeably, since we do not really mind that much about semantics.

The Egyptian Mysterie Schools were established around 10,000 BCE—just after the fall of Atlantis—by our ancestors: a tribe that had escaped the sinking continent. They brought their teachings, healing tools, and other technologies with them to Iyrgr—the New Earth, which you now call Egypt. The Mysteries were part of everyday life in Egypt for a long time. This time is known as the golden age of Egypt. Although the schools were destroyed thousands of years ago, we will explain the school system as if it is still vibrant and operating. From our higher perspective in the spiritual realms, the schools still exist, because they are so much a part of many souls' memories—and are therefore now imprinted on the universal soul.

―

The Mystical Schools are centers of healing and places of training for spiritual enlightenment. Our schools accept initiates from far and wide, without prejudice or favor. When initiates begin their training, they are permitted to wear dark kohl around their eyes and on their eyebrow bones. This is in remembrance of some of the original teachers of the Egyptian Mysteries, the Hathors, upon whom these darkened features naturally appear.

It is a great honor to be accepted into the Mysterie Schools. The entrance tests are stringent and impersonal. Students who have been accepted into the schools wear their kohl daily with pride. If at any time they are no longer part of the schools, they must cease to wear the kohl. The eyes of kohl are symbolic of an individual's personal desire to seek an enlightened reason for being. The eyes, as the gateway to the soul, are enlivened as initiates journey into the mysteries of their own souls—and therefore into life itself. The outside world refers to our initiates as *seekers* or *sedjaters*.

Following the mystical path is not for everybody. Some only wish to learn the foundations of spirituality, while others have no interest in spiritual growth at all. We do not advertise our schools, nor do we actively recruit initiates. People whose souls desire spiritual development or enlightenment naturally gravitate towards the schools. Our school system has been designed by the ancients of our order to facilitate those who wish to grow towards illumination. For individuals who feel no desire to follow a spiritual path, we hold no judgement or opinion. The work of the schools is wholly accepting of all humanity, and we celebrate the differences of humankind on their journey of evolutionary ascension.

Some individuals might only do a term's schooling, or a few years, and then leave the schools to join society at large. Others may complete many of the lessons, qualifying as masters or *pharas*. Only a few continue to completion and become inducted as *phararohs* or *pharaohs*. Beyond this point, the pharaohs may remain within the Mysteries as priests/priestesses, in turn teaching all they have learnt to initiates. Those who transcend the school system altogether, but continue to grow in illumination according to a dedicated spiritual path, are called high-priests/high-priestesses. The high-priests/high-priestesses can choose to remain in the schools, or they can move into a life external to the school system.

There is no time stipulation placed on the attainment of mastery or priesthood. Some individuals are born with a high state of awareness from previous lifetimes of spiritual learning. They might ascend rapidly through the Mysterie School lessons and attain mastery within a few decades. Others, who are fairly new to the Mysteries, might take an entire lifetime just for the first few lessons. Souls, whose chosen path is a spiritual one, will return lifetime after lifetime to the schools in order to continue their lessons. Although all life is in essence spiritual, we consider a soul who is on a spiritual path to be one who continually seeks a higher degree of spiritual mastery and understanding within life—often with the intention of expanding and passing on this knowledge to others.

The entrance examination for the schools is mostly an objective one and is conducted by the priests/priestesses. A potential student is put through several energetic testing processes that measure his or her level of spiritual consciousness and state of readiness for the school system. The entrance examination is actually a series of tests, using methods such as kinesiological testing, also known as body-response testing; chakra activation levels measured with energy rods and dowsing wands; sound testing with tuning forks and other instruments; color and light therapy testing and iridology; crystal analyses; a personal interview; and body language assessment. Over the years, the mechanisms for entrance examinations change, but those listed are some of the main methods used to test the eligibility of potential students. We will expand upon the testing processes in the following chapters, since they are used consistently for all manner of analyses throughout the school system and specifically for initiations.

The tests are objective in the sense that neither the student nor the priest/priestess doing the testing can manipulate the results in any way. For example, the energy rod, when brought into close contact with the physical body at the spinal column and then struck on a resonation surface, will release a vibratory sound of a particular chord or pitch. This sound resonates with the frequency at which the individual is operating, according to his or her overall energetic chakra system. A less evolved individual will be most in tune with the bottom chakras, and therefore resonate at a lower frequency—and so the sound released will be of a lower pitch. A more spiritually, and therefore energetically, advanced individual will naturally resonate at a higher pitch with the higher chakras. No individual is admitted to the schools whose overall frequency is less than that of the fourth, or heart, chakra. (The chakra system is explained further in chapters 3 and 7.)

Should the potential students fail their entrance exams, they are provided with recommendations on how they can raise their energetic, or consciousness, level within life to the point where they would be accepted into the schools. (The relationship between consciousness and energy is explained further in the following chapter.) An individual who genuinely wants to become an initiate will eventually reach a suitably high energetic vibration to enter the schools. It is all about commitment to the spiritual path.

We would like to explain the difference between the level of consciousness of a person and the degree of enlightenment or illumination. Consciousness is more of a mental learning procedure that can be taught and that the soul can carry from lifetime to lifetime. Enlightenment, however, needs to be experienced; it is the *doing* of consciousness. The level of consciousness can never retrogress. But if souls are not living their particular luminosities (awareness levels), then they are living in an unenlightened manner. For example, two souls may be born with the same degree of consciousness potential, which is a spiritual measure of what they are capable of achieving in a lifetime. The consciousness measure is entirely based on overall soul potential. Attaining enlightenment, however, is the active process of putting that potential to use. One of the souls may achieve awareness through proactively pursuing a spiritual path, while the other may not. The soul who actively engages in spiritual application moves closer towards illumination, while the other soul stays still and does not evolve spiritually—or evolves far more slowly. However, their consciousness potentials have not changed and are still equal.

The difference between consciousness and enlightenment may be likened to a bigger picture and a smaller picture. The bigger picture is the level of consciousness. So, for example, all human souls may be blessed with the same level of consciousness potential at a point in time. This consciousness potential can be raised, but only with a group effort. The smaller picture is the level of illumination. The humans occupying Earth will be at vastly different levels of enlightenment, and it is entirely up to individuals to work on their own progress.

Since the level of enlightenment of an individual corresponds directly to his or her overall energy vibration, the energetic testing processes are designed to measure enlightenment rather than consciousness.

Although consciousness and enlightenment are linked, the consciousness potential of an individual doesn't often change within a lifetime, whereas her progress towards illumination should increase with her spiritual evolution, if she is on track. If consciousness can be likened to a ladder with a finite height, the level of enlightenment is the particular step upon which a person is placed. The ladder is more often described within the Mysterie Schools as a pyramid that contains an ascending energy spiral of illumination. (This will be explained in more detail in chapter 2.)

While we generally differentiate between consciousness and illumination, we also know that your societies use the words interchangeably, along with other words for spiritual awareness. Therefore, please do not become too concerned with these technical differences, since they were only raised in preparation for later chapters. We would prefer that you understand spiritual development at a heart level and secondarily at an intellectual level. So call it what you will and know that whatever terms we refer to in this book are what you believe them to be at the time of reading. If you would like to think of spiritual ascension as a single, simplistic concept, please do so.

⏷

It is important that individuals are at a certain level in their spiritual evolution before beginning the mystical lessons of the Mysterie Schools. We have found through experience that students entering the schools prematurely are easily overwhelmed and more likely to fail. Also, it is important that we reduce the spreading of misconceptions by those who have left the system. Many individuals come back lifetime after lifetime to complete their training, which explains why some pass the entrance exams easily and others are turned away until they become ready.

The way of the Mysteries is not the path for everybody, and we go to great lengths to keep the lessons secret. This secrecy is not an attempt to control the sacred knowledge of the schools but rather exists because the information needs to be taught within context, in a structured and systematic way. Certain aspects must be understood before others are revealed. It is the way of the universe, and so it is the way of our school system. Communicating some of the very advanced material to non-initiates, or those students who are not ready for the information, is dangerous and confusing for all concerned. Therefore, the sacred teachings are protected—not because we wish to dominate these truths—but because we have learned, over many ages, the best way to teach and communicate mystical knowledge—and so we have been entrusted by universal forces with its transference.

Throughout this text, we will be taking you through some of the concepts of our Mystical Schools. We have carefully selected what we think might be most interesting to humankind at this time. The book includes information from various levels of learning within the school system, but we have been careful with what has been revealed and what has not. We are forever bound to uphold the sacredness and mysterie of universal knowledge. However, we also teach that all universal knowledge is available to everybody at all times—if they simply learn how to access it. If you become frustrated because we have not told you something you would like to know, continue to seek with a true heart, and you will find your answers—perhaps through acquired knowledge and perhaps through life experience. Although we protect the pathways of the Pharonic Mystical Schools, and all the subsidiaries of these, we are not the keepers of universal reality—nobody is.

We hope you have fun with this information and that it awakens some memory in you, of when you perhaps were an initiate yourself. We have faith that your curiosity will take you on your own journey of illumination.

This is an ovoculum
of our high-alphabet;
it means Faith.

# 2
# The Pyramid and the Energy Spiral

Humankind's journey upon Earth is likened to a pyramid. In order to ascend in spiritual mastery, there are four aspects to perfect within the physical manifestation of human life. These are like the four corners of the base of a pyramid: the *ka*, personal energy vibration; the *ra*, relational connection to others; the *ptah*, service to all humanity and life; and the *phah*, connection to nature and the elements.

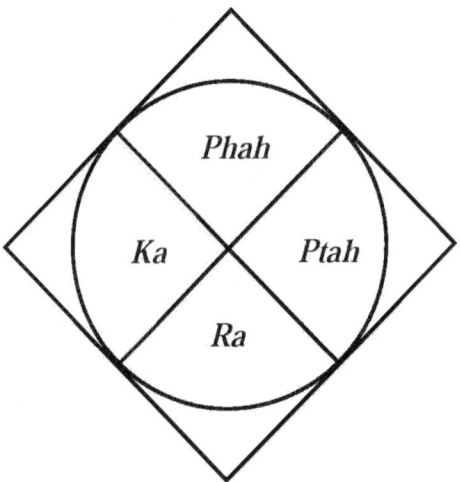

The top of the pyramid is considered the highest level of consciousness an individual, or a group of individuals, can achieve within life. We also refer to this highest state of being as absolute spiritual enlightenment, illumination, or mastery. Progression to this point of awareness is likened to an ascending energy spiral, in which an individual grows in enlightenment towards the highest potential of his spiritual consciousness. As a person focuses on each of the four aspects of personal growth—the ka, ra, ptah, and phah—in a balanced way, his energy consciousness moves up in a spiral wave.

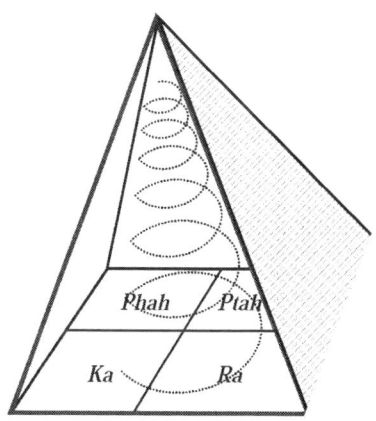

An increase in the enlightenment levels of an individual is a personal journey towards the apex of the pyramid—also known as the highest state of awareness that she is able to achieve as a spiritual being. The top of the pyramid represents a particular level of consciousness, or highest potential, which is a reflection of a collective journey. This apex may be raised to infinite levels as a group of souls ascends.

Similarly, individuals ascend up the energy spiral in an infinite journey. They are born with a certain conscious potential, which we can think of as the pyramidal structure. Ideally, they should ascend up the pyramid as their levels of enlightenment increase by following the energy spiral. Should they reach the apex of the pyramid and attain enlightenment, they will discover the secret that expands the pyramid to infinite levels. This will be discussed further in the final chapter, but we advise you not to skip to it now.

▼

The raising of potential consciousness is a universal concept and may be extended to include the cosmos. As an example, let us look at a group of human beings on the Earth. There may be billions of souls incarnated in human form and living human lives. Let us say that all but one of these billions of souls have reached a particular point in consciousness. They are all vibrating at a certain level of awareness, except for one individual who might be stuck somewhere on the upward spiral. The result is that the whole of humanity cannot ascend to a higher level. In other words, the top of humanity's collective pyramid is stuck at a certain, unmovable point. This one individual is delaying the ascension of all humanity.

Continuing with the example, let us move our perspective outwards to the universe in which the Earth exists. The Earth is part of a cosmic system that contains a multitude of life-forms existing at a multitude of levels of spiritual consciousness. All of these life-forms may have reached a certain level of consciousness but are waiting for the inhabitants of the Earth planet to achieve their own particular level of illumination before they, in turn, can consider that the whole of their universe has attained a certain level. In this case, only when the human beings of the Earth planet have collectively reached their pinnacle can the entire universe be considered ready to jointly expand the top of the cosmic pyramid and continue with universal evolution.

So our one individual on Earth, who is holding up humanity's ascension, is in effect delaying the ascension of the universe at large. That is why it is so important for each of us to do our utmost to reach the ascension point. Those destined to teach must fulfill their purpose by helping others reach the ascension point. One of the universal laws sounds something like this: *When all beings (humans) are vibrating at their highest possible potentials at a point in time, then group consciousness may ascend to a higher state of being.* This applies to all scales of existence—from a small family living on planet Earth, to all human beings, to all universal life-forms. There are no limits to where the universal rules apply.

Spiritual mastery is ultimately a group effort. Individuals may be commended for reaching illumination themselves, but it is not enough. Unless they connect with the group consciousness around them, and aspire to raise others to their level, their individual journey will end there. The initiates of the Mysteries learn this through experience. After decades or lifetimes of focusing intently on their own progress towards illumination, they must do all they can from the plateau of understanding to raise all others in awareness. By connecting with the group consciousness, the student is connecting with universal consciousness; everything is One.

The path taken by the initiates through the school system has been designed to be symbolic of life. The journey into the Mysteries is not supposed to take anything away from material life—or replace it. When the schools existed, certain parts of human reality were still in their infancy, particularly the human emotions on a collective level. In your modern-day, however, accelerating spiritual momentum has caused human emotions to evolve to a high degree in a short time. The Mysterie Schools were originally designed to facilitate the earthly journeys of the most advanced souls who could not get the experiences they required for spiritual ascension within the mundane, material world on Earth. Since the schools were destroyed, chaos and unpredictability on the planet have increased, but so has the Earth's potential to act as a spiritual training ground.

Returning to the methods of the Mysterie School students: their spiritual lessons emulate life experience and convey divine knowledge so that they can work progressively on their ka, ra, ptah, and phah. These four aspects are referred to within the schools as the Four Teachers of Life or simply as the Four Teachers. Collectively, these Four Teachers are known by the mystical name of Ra-Harakhty. The symbolic representation of Ra-Harakhty is the falcon, also known as Horus. Horus the falcon is an animation symbol that holds the promise of what is possible when mastery is achieved.

The Four Teachers—personal energy vibration; relationship to others; service to humanity and life; and the elemental connection—need to be developed to their highest degree by the initiates. They are the foundation concepts of the pyramid. As the students practice and achieve awareness in these four quadrants of earthly life, their levels of energetic enlightenment move upwards in a spiral pattern, forming the shape of a pyramid. However, each one of the four concepts cannot receive undue attention, because it is the actualization of an equilibrium between all these aspects of human divinity that will eventually guide the initiate towards mastery. Only when the ka, ra, ptah, and phah are acting in harmony does an alchemical change occur within the energetic body of the student, and he begins to see more clearly a pathway to further ascension and ultimate illumination—the top of the pyramid.

The initiates are guided to work consciously towards the top of the pyramid, and the attainment of their own illumination—also known as self-mastery or *nevana*. When the student has ultimately mastered the Four Teachers, she has achieved Ra-Harakhty and exists in a constant state of balance. When this balance can be maintained, it means that the four pillars of ka, ra, ptah, and phah are acting as the foundation quadrants for spiritual development. Maintaining the harmony of Ra-Harakhty is an absolute method of reaching illumination within due course.

Achieving Ra-Harakhty is not necessarily the same thing as reaching illumination, but illumination cannot be achieved without Ra-Harakhty. Once an initiate has attained balance between the Four Teachers, this balance must be maintained and developed, in order to reach ultimate illumination and the state of nevana. This is the permanent experience of illumination, whereas Ra-Harakhty is the process of balancing the four foundation energies of the pyramid; it can be experienced at any point on ascension up the pyramid—in fact, Ra-Harakhty is the requirement for ascension up the pyramid.

The pharaohs are depicted in glyphs as rising from a pyramid so that they appear to be wearing pointed skirts or pleated dresses. The skirts and robes emulate the shape of a pyramid so that the pharaohs seem to be ascending from the very structure itself and are transcending the pyramid's apex. This means that they have attained absolute mastery, the top of the pyramid, and so transcend it; in that transcension they become the very object to which they were ascending—they become the pyramid. The pyramid is the universal representation of cosmic light; it is ultimate illumination. (See image in chapter 11 under the Pleated-Skirt item.)

The actual initiation process for this state of illumination is conducted inside one of the three great pyramids on the Negeb (Nile) plateau. We explain this initiation process more fully in chapter 9.

▼

Since we will not be explaining actual methods of spiritual development within this book, we will not provide information on how to establish ka, ra, ptah, and phah. Although the initiates are carefully guided towards building the four pillars of the energy spiral, achievement of Ra-Harakhty is ultimately a personal journey. There are certain techniques and practices that assist in moving closer to self-mastery, but initiates are required to find their own way up the energy spiral.

Now we will explain ka, ra, ptah, and phah a little further.

The ka is the personal energy vibration or energy twin of a person. It is the energetic body that is a manifestation of the soul personality and the container of creative potential in life. The ka is indestructible and is linked to, but is not, the soul. It fuels the manifested body mostly from a spiritual dimension. Although the ka is not wholly part of the physical body, when it is depleted the physical body will suffer. A powerful ka is necessary for healthy relationships.

The ra is the interchange between individuals and their surroundings—specifically their relationships with others. A healthy ra exists as a continual flow of energy that is both given and received. It is an energy exchange. This does not mean that packets of energy are literally exchanged between people and objects. Ra more specifically refers to the condition of the energetic space between people and things—between their separateness. This energetic flow reflects the type and quality of their relationship. An individual's ra is also indicated by the kinds of company, situations, and environments that they attract. Healthy ra is necessary for development of ptah.

Ptah is the humbling of the self to divine service, which is given through the self but is not necessarily of the self. Ptah is the opening of the personal physical vessel to universal forces that desire to work through the individual. The individual becomes an instrument for divine spiritual work whose attainment may be measured through the heart-center or what your societies commonly refer to as passion. The ptah is achieved when the personal drives of the individual match those requirements of universal forces exactly. Some of you may refer to this as a calling. The ptah opens the human vessel in order to achieve phah.

Attaining phah requires an ongoing connection to the forces of nature. Human beings are an intricate part of the Earth's natural environment. Driven intellectually, most modern humans strive to separate from the natural structures and rhythms of the planet. This is dangerous, and analogous to cutting a baby's umbilical cord before birth. People are nature, and developing a vital phah is essential for building the ka.

Ultimately, the ka, ra, ptah, and phah are all mutually dependent upon one another—fingers and toes of the same organism. Underdevelopment of one of the four quadrants leads to retardation of overall Ra-Harakhty and therefore stagnation of ascension up the energy spiral of the metaphorical pyramid of illumination.

# 3
# The Ladder of Lessons and the Djed-Column

As we have explained, the lessons of the Mysteries are designed to emulate life. However, we naturally need to give some structure to the school system through which the initiates might progress during their years in the Mystical Schools. The number seven applies to many of our lessons and is considered sacred. Therefore, seven distinctive levels of learning have been formulated over the years. Each level has its own name and own particular set of lessons that the students are required to master. There is a dual procedure that occurs when the student moves from one level to another.

First, there is an initiation process that is mostly qualitative, or subjective, in nature. The initiation occurs once a particular level has been completed and the initiate desires to move to the next level. If the initiate does not desire to move up a level, then the initiation is not performed and they may leave the school system willingly. The qualitative initiation is designed mostly for the higher-self of the initiates. The higher-self is the eternal essence of a person that remains in the spiritual realm during life. Ideally, the higher-self should guide an individual's activities in life and assist the soul to reach its highest potential.

The qualitative initiation both activates the higher-self and confirms that the path being followed is correct. In other words, the initiation says to the higher-self, "Hey, I am moving up a level; is this okay?" Should this be amenable to the overall soul development at that point in time, then the student should pass through the qualitative initiation with enjoyment and pleasure, feeling a security in the decision to continue his or her studies. Should the higher-self not wish to move forward in the mystical direction at that particular point in time, then the initiation may be an uncomfortable experience in which the student faces many doubts. Either way, the decision to move through the qualitative initiation belongs entirely to the student.

We may not reveal the procedures and practices for these qualitative initiations because they are entirely mystical in nature and delicately contextual to the initiation processes. We can only say that there are certain routine procedures for various initiations, but these are usually accompanied by procedures tailored to maximize a specific individual's numinous experience.

The second type of initiation is objective and is conducted in tandem with (or generally around the same time period as) the subjective initiation. This initiation is more quantitative in nature and seeks to measure the energetic readiness, or state of enlightenment, of the students. We have various methods to test the progress of the initiates' ascension up the energy spiral. These mostly include those metaphysical methods mentioned in chapter 1, which seek to attain information in a manner beyond the limits of the mundane human senses and intellect.

Not all of the objective testing mechanisms are used for a single initiation. There are tests to decide what initiatory procedures should be used for each student as they move up a level of learning.

## The Ladder of Lessons and the Djed-Column

For instance, when initiates begin the school system, they are all subject to the same testing procedures. At higher levels, initiates are likely to be tested via a range of methods that have been chosen specifically for them. Although the group of tests might be different for each individual as they move up the ladder of lessons, the results remain objective, fair, and accurate. Certain initiations, such as trans-meditation, are experienced by all students required to move (in this case) from Level 4 to Level 5. Trans-meditation within the great pyramids is also a requirement for completion of Level 7.

All of the testing methods have been used for thousands of years, and many of the testing instruments (specifically the energy rods and crystals) were brought to Egypt via Atlantis. Our ancestors also brought templates and materials to create the various tools we need within the Mysterie Schools. These include: musical and sound instruments, hieroglyphics, sculpting, and masonry.

The priests and priestesses who conduct the initiations and tests are expertly trained in the methods required. They often have exclusive use of the sacred tools, instruments, and materials needed to perform various actions. The selfsame methods used for testing may be used in healing procedures to rapidly raise the vibratory energetic levels of initiates. This specifically refers to the crystals, energy rods, and sound instruments, and will be explained further in later chapters.

The objective initiation is so called because the testers may not manipulate or subjectivize the results in any way. The results are what they are, and if an initiate passes the objective testing, then that is final. Even if the priests/priestesses believe that an initiate is not ready to continue up the ladder of lessons, once initiates pass the quantitative initiation it is entirely their decision to continue with the Mysteries. If a student is not naturally ready to continue, it is hoped that they will come to this realization independently during the qualitative initiation.

Initiates are never forced, or even urged, to complete lessons or to achieve a certain level of learning. However, if they show promise, they are gently guided by the priests and priestesses as they continue. Beyond Level 5, students are considered too advanced to be encouraged at all. From this point onwards, initiates achieve a much higher degree of independence, similar to your modern university systems; individuals must make a conscious and independent choice to be schooled.

⬇

The student's ascension up the ladder of lessons is likened to the ascension up the energy spiral. The levels of learning are designed to guide the student towards enlightenment. As explained previously, there is a difference between consciousness and illumination. Whereas consciousness is the *knowing,* illumination is the *being.* A person can be fully conscious and aware of what level she is on, while at the same time her degree of illumination is lagging. This is normal because energy flows where awareness goes. The initiate needs to be aware that she wants to attain illumination before she can actually get there. While consciousness is fairly intangible and is processed through the mind, illumination is wholly an energetic ascension process and can therefore be measured in the objective initiation procedures. Illumination is described as a level of enlightenment—or literally the amount of light a body can hold. Increasing illumination is an alchemical process as every cell of the body transforms to absorb and hold increasing amounts of light. The measurement of enlightenment is therefore objective and absolute; it corresponds exactly to the particular level of learning on which a student finds themselves.

Of course, the repeating number seven is important in this process because ascension up the ladder of lessons, associated with increasing enlightenment, corresponds to the seven energy chakras of the human as well as the Seven Rays (explained further in chapters 7 and 8). The names of the levels of learning are given below, but they may appear strange to you. Since the Mysteries were brought to Egypt from Atlantis, many of the terms are also part of that previous civilization—specifically the Atlantian tribe that settled Iyrgr. The naming of the levels derives in most cases from the complexes that housed the students of a particular level, except for Level 6, which is self-explanatory, and Level 7, which means *activation*.

## Ladder of Lessons—Period Names and Brief Overview

Level 1—*The Fedulca Period*: Orientation and introduction into the Mysteries.

Level 2—*The Ribotome*: Activation of the energy centers and attunement with sound, light, color, and magnetism/electromagnetism.

Level 3—*Bidanga*: Introduction to the healing arts and alchemical physics. The human body (not only the physical body).

Level 4—*Inniswayo*: Integration of all other lessons and initiation into trans-meditation. The initiate becomes a phara, a master. Activation of the first three Rays would have been attained by Level 4.

Level 5—*Hedulgo*: Refinement of the healing arts. Specialization in a chosen field. Activation of the fourth Ray, the heart energy-center.

Level 6—*Omnipresence*: Activation of the fifth Ray, the creative energy-center, in preparation for *Octivio*. Continuation with specializations.

Level 7—*Octivio*: Activation of the sixth and seventh Rays (the psychic and spiritual energy-centers) and initiation into the universal order through the pyramid initiation via trans-meditation. The initiate becomes a pharaoh, a teacher of the light, and may remain in the school system as an instructing priest/priestess if he or she desires.

Those who choose to remain within the school system once their priest/priestess calling is complete are considered high-priests/priestesses. From then on, even if the high-priests/priestesses leave the school system, they will always retain their titles. Their Mysterie practices and experiences are considered to have taken them beyond the physical life, and they are part of the universal system of Masters that exists beyond life on Earth.

# The Ladder of Lessons and the Djed-Column

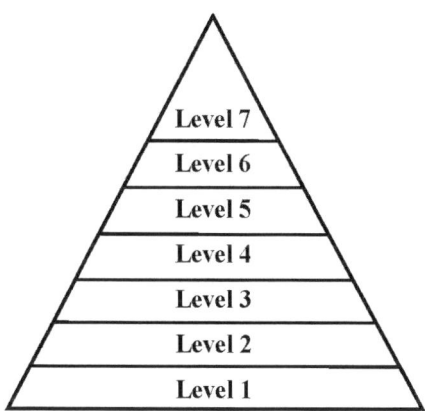

As the students progress up the ladder of lessons, the learning becomes more profound. We don't like to use the word *difficult* because the tests are not necessarily harder—instead they become deeper, more customized, subtler, and longer lasting. Not only do the lessons become more specific, but the time taken to master each subsequent level is exponentially greater. For instance, Level 1 may take one to two years, but Level 5 might take ten years. This is in the case of a highly evolved soul. Younger souls are likely to take thousands of lifetimes just to get to the point where they would be accepted into the school system. Even advanced souls will take numerous incarnations to get through the levels, and moving beyond the pyramidal structure to ultimate illumination is rare on your planet Earth. If you count up all the avatars and masters you are aware of over the last few thousand years of Earth's history, you will realize this.

Also, once a student reaches Level 5 and beyond, his learning begins to include more experiences from real, organic life rather than from the scholarly structure of the temple schools. The students are not informed of this by the priests/priestesses, however. While they are given ever more freedom to join the real world outside of the Mysterie Schools, their integrity and commitment to their spiritual path is being increasingly tested.

Should students move out completely into the material world and forget their learning, they have failed the next level. The greatest test of the Mysteries lies in a student's ability to interact fully in the ordinary world in full cognizance of their spirituality, of who they are, and why they are alive. In time, they will realize that in truth there is no difference between the internal world of the schools and the external world of the non-initiated. They will know that they are truly free and that their commitment to their spiritual path is a choice, albeit a choice that makes their life's work intensely meaningful and more successful.

In this way, the schools are designed to be a true reflection of life—not separate from the mundane—but rather a colorful reminder of the existence of humanity and each individual soul's purpose within life. The Mysterie Schools are designed primarily to help certain individuals, those who choose to do so, to develop towards self-mastery and ultimately to a mastery of life. It requires a deep and lasting commitment and dedication to the soul's true path. It is an easy concept to understand but a difficult one to master. The distractions created by the individual's ego within everyday life are numerous; when combined with the group mentalities of society, they are near-impossible to overcome without a high level of mastery.

Therefore, from about Level 5, the constant guidance of the Mysterie School priests/priestesses is gradually replaced by tests in which the initiates must make choices independently for themselves. The initiates are not made aware of this change in methods, because it is part of their learning that they are able to transfer good decisions into their daily lives without assistance from others. It is a true test of their level of awakening. It is also from Level 5 that the dropout rate for initiates becomes very high. Some of the students consciously make the decision to drift away from the schools at this time. Others, whose spiritual potential is promising, and who are often aiming for priesthood, persevere past Level 5. However, because the Mysteries become more personal and abstract at this point, some individuals from this second group begin to fail their lessons unconsciously and become increasingly removed from the true path of the Mysteries.

The attainment of Level 7—ultimate consciousness or illumination—is regarded as a never-ending state of being in which the levels of learning almost become redundant. Once initiated into Level 7, students reach the point of awareness where the lessons that have guided them are secondary to their skill in applying themselves to the greater school of life. They are free to move about in the world, in a life that they have chosen, but in full conscious illumination. They are fully aware of who they are and why they are alive; they actively participate in this life while remaining eternally connected to the divine and their higher-self. The continuation of this elevated state of being, and the application of correct life decisions for their soul, is the true and final test of the Mysteries—the completion and mastery of Level 7.

Once initiated into Level 7, the person is called a phara-roh, or a pharaoh. At this level, individuals know whether they are destined for a life within the Mysterie Schools or outside of the system that brought them to this point. Either way, it is the choice of their souls, and they are aware of the choice and embrace it. Those who, in a fully conscious state, gravitate to life outside of the schools after completing Level 7 will remain equipped with the spiritual tools that they learnt in the Mysteries to guide them for life. They are neither separated from nor unaware of their spirituality—it is a continually evolving part of themselves as they move through their chosen life. Those who choose to remain in the schools generally press on to priesthood/priestesshood and possibly even further to high-priesthood/high-priestesshood. However, facilitating mystical knowledge as a teacher within the schools is a personal choice, not a natural progression.

Although the pyramid initiation marks the completion of Level 7, the true test of having passed or failed the final level is a pharaoh's ability to maintain his or her spiritual path. The great mysterie of the school system is that life itself is the great initiator. The schools simply prepare and facilitate a structured path towards the initiations of life. This is never explained to the students—ever. Once they have passed from the school system, it becomes their prerogative to make good decisions in line with their soul's higher purpose. The pyramid initiation lays the foundation for deep insight into what would constitute good decisions, because by completion of Level 7 the students will know their earthly purpose. (This is discussed further in chapter 9.)

Level 7 is also the stage at which the pharaohs become wholly a part of the universal order and offer themselves up to the cosmic kharmic testing process. Hereafter, the true test becomes the students' battle against themselves—their will versus the desires of their higher-selves. If they work in accordance with their higher-selves, and therefore the overall god-energy, then they have passed the school of life. If they make poor decisions that work against themselves, and therefore against god, then they have failed in life. There is no further direct guidance from the schools post Level 7—the pharaohs are now part of a much higher order of schooling in which only they can be the judges.

⏷

As students progress up the Mysterie School ladder of lessons, their spiritual consciousness is spiraling up towards mastery. If they are not growing in consciousness, they will not pass the energetic initiatory tests. If initiates do not pass an initiatory test, they have the choice to try again or to leave the school system. What they are never told is that the key to passing the tests lies in their true desire to ascend up the spiral of consciousness. The tests are designed to emulate life; and the individual's belief that spiritual mastery is separate from material life is an illusion. If initiates choose to stay and persevere, sooner or later, they will pass the test—this is a universal law. *What a person desires to be—will be.* The law does not give particulars on how that desire might manifest, or how long it will take, because the details and degree of determination are up to the individual's higher-self.

If initiates choose to leave the school system, they are making a soul choice at a very deep level. This choice is probably that they will attain spiritual mastery at another time—most likely in another lifetime. However, let us not give the impression that mastery takes a single lifetime. Most souls experience thousands (in fact hundreds of thousands) of incarnations until they reach illumination. The Mysterie Schools are designed to organize and hasten this spiritual learning. The school process is designed for the soul's own good. Left to their own devices, souls can go around and around in circles, lifetime after lifetime, without making much progress.

No judgement is passed by the priests/priestesses if students leave the school system. It is understood that there is a time for everything, and not everybody is ready for certain levels of spiritual development in the same way at the same time. However, it is also a fact that sooner or later, every soul must attain a particular level of enlightenment or be left behind in the evolutionary process. The Mysterie Schools are not the only method of attaining spiritual enlightenment, but they are a tried-and-true path to discovery of the self and attainment of self-mastery.

⬇

At this juncture, we need to introduce the concept of the Djed-column. The Djed-column is the internal metaphysical structure within each human being, in which peace may reside if duality is mastered. The Djed is likened to a four-tiered tower in which the physical, mental, emotional, and spiritual aspects operate harmoniously in balance. The column is the metaphysical pathway of spiritual energy that resonates within each human being and, if healthy, is a continually moving upward current of conscious energy. This energy passes through each of the chakra centers on its way through the crown and to an everlasting connection to the divine—or the universal source-energy. The Djed-column needs to be developed as a prerequisite for students to move up the ladder of lessons, but it is an aspect of mastery that is attained in a personal way outside of the structured lessons.

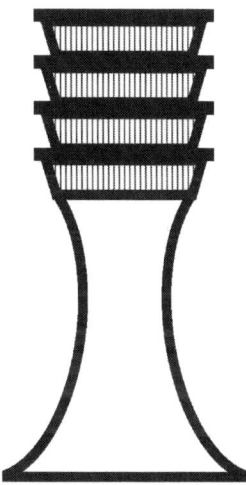

**A diagram of the Djed-column or Djed-pillar.**

The Djed—which means a healthy, vibrant core or foundation in our language—is a key concept for progress through the seven lessons of learning and ascension up the energy spiral. The Djed-column is the internal house of stillness, or temple, within each human being where the continual presence of god may be attained. Spiritually, this holy space is a state of highly conscious existence in which the initiate is able to balance all his or her energy centers and at the same time connect with the divine. All things are within balance when the Djed is attained: duality is balanced (light and dark forces), the energy centers are healthy and active, Ra-Harakhty is in motion, and the individual's personal energy vibration continues on its upward spiral—no longer able to dip below a certain level of consciousness. In other words, the initiate has passed the point of no return and is destined to either maintain a relatively high level of enlightenment or, more likely, to continue growing in everlasting consciousness.

The Djed-column is comparable to the structural space in our temples known as the *inner sanctum, holy cryptorium,* or *initiatory crypt*. This is a holy space, which usually exists in physical form as the most internal sanctum or room of the temple. Students are required to work on their own physical, mental, emotional, and spiritual states in private until they have developed a healthy Djed. Attaining the Djed is one of the requirements of reaching Level 4 and becoming a phara. The initiatory crypt is a space to which only students past phara level may be admitted. Within the inner sanctum, the initiate practices to attune directly with god. This may be the god of themselves (their higher-selves), or some other energy that is available for guidance and inspiration. Either way, the Djed-column and the inner sanctum are the pathways to communication with the voice within and therefore with the universal divine.

Finding harmony through the Djed-column may sound like a simple concept, but continually living in a state of harmony on the physical, mental, emotional, and spiritual planes is a great achievement for a human being. This is because human beings are incarnated as dualistic creatures in which bipolar destructive and creative forces are in continual tension.

By connecting to the divine through the Djed-column, initiates become a tool for god's work in life; by operating through the Djed they are able to attain a sense of permanency in all-that-is. In other words, they recognize themselves as a part of the cosmic whole, and they can go forth and conduct divine work as thoroughly conscious beings who resonate at the highest spiritual levels. The ego has dissolved and the spiritual nature rules their activities and decisions. They are living examples of the all-creative god-energy, working towards the highest good of all.

The Djed-column is a mutually inclusive concept; many facets of the Mysteries such as the energy spiral and Ra-Harakhty, the healing arts, trans-meditation and many of the school lessons, are designed to develop the Djed. The Djed in turn supports all other facets of the Mysteries and ultimately becomes like a *column that supports pillars that are supporting the column*. The Djed-column is like spiritual scaffolding that facilitates all other spiritual development.

Therefore, when we examine the structure of our holy physical temples, the inner sanctum is placed in the middle of the buildings, often surrounded by pillars. This sanctum, or cryptorium, is a metaphysical gateway to the Source and representative of the central energetic structure of the human being. It is easiest for initiates to connect deeply to the divine through this inner crypt. However, if they are advanced enough energetically, they should be able to connect to the divine at any place and at any time. The initiatory crypt is provided both as a symbolic representation of the importance of creating an internal, permanent platform for the god-energy, as well as a sacred physical space that facilitates the attainment of a divine connection to god through meditation and prayer.

When initiates are truly connected to the Source, their energy bodies will vibrate at the highest frequency possible for a physically incarnated being—at the seventh Ray. In this state, initiates are considered to be a living entity of flame, a facilitator for the god-energy in physical manifestation. Creative universal forces are able to work through them, and their physical bodies are simply vessels for the divine. However, it is attainment of the Djed—the divine balance between physical, mental, emotional, and spiritual states—that is necessary for this soul union.

In chapter 7, we will discuss the auratic colombine, which is a similar concept to the Djed-column in terms of being a metaphysical structure that facilitates spiritual development. The main difference, however, is that the Djed exists only during physical manifestation while the auratic colombine is part of the soul imprint beyond life and therefore ever-present. While the colombine is an essential illuminating connection to all-that-is, the Djed-column is like an energetic backbone that human beings may develop during their incarnations but that dissolves upon physical death.

There are a few glyph representations for the Djed-column. The basic structure (as above) is a four-tiered tower—the four levels indicating achievement of balance and harmony on the physical, mental, emotional, and spiritual planes.

The tower also may be reproduced as a platform on the head of an individual. This is representative of how humans contain the Djed-column within their beings, hidden from view. The mystical platform at their crowns shows that they are prepared for whatever the universe has to bring them or require of them. In this sense, the Djed-column is popping-out from their heads, ready to support further development.

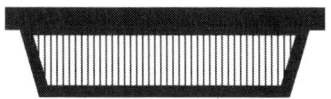

**A diagram of the Djed-platform. There is also an image of the Djed-platform in chapter 11, *Representations of Initiations Passed*, below the Matted Wig item.**

The platform is further explained in chapter 11, under the Crowns item, because it serves as a metaphorical adornment. The Djed-platform also mimics a resonator box, which is a wooden box that amplifies sound instruments, particularly tuning-fork resonators. The value of sound within the schools is explained fully in chapter 8.

An image of an initiatory crypt (small temple room with two pillars) may be placed on this mystical platform to show an active connection to the god-energy as well as a life in continual service and devotion to all-that-is.

The structure of the Djed-column is a universal concept and is used in many of the world's traditions, where it may take on slightly different meanings. The Djed is also a physical structure in the Akashic Temple, in which the soul records of all universal beings are kept. Also, the inner sanctum of the great pyramids—or trans-meditative pyramids—is arranged as a Djed-column. Below the internal tower of four granite slabs plus a granite cap, the initiates attain deep meditation inside their sarcophagi. (Akasha and trans-meditation are explained in chapter 9.)

The animation symbol for the Djed-column is two intertwined snakes. One is black and one is gold. They spiral around one another from tip to snout, and their faces meet infinitesimally close together. The gold serpent has a black stripe above its eye and the black serpent has a gold stripe above its eye. Together, they are the perfect image of balance and duality. These two snakes are so profoundly mystical and sacred to our traditions that they are rarely inscribed, but they remain a meditation symbol for the initiates who have awakened to their presence.

Various representations are associated with the students' progress up the levels of learning and the associated initiations. Some are worn as clothing or accessories; others are reserved for the stone glyphs and statues only. *The Representations of Initiations Passed* are discussed further in chapter 11.

# 4
# The Sacred Elementals and the Alchemy of Spirit

The four sacred elements are *Re, Ay, Shu,* and *Ney.* They are considered real beings that are particular manifestations of spirit energy. In combinations, these four sacred elements, or elementals, give rise to everything that exists in life—whether organic or inorganic. human beings—and all life on Earth and in the universe—are constituted of elemental energy. Correspondingly, all life is a part of the elemental energies. Life and human beings are indivisible from the elementals—always and forever.

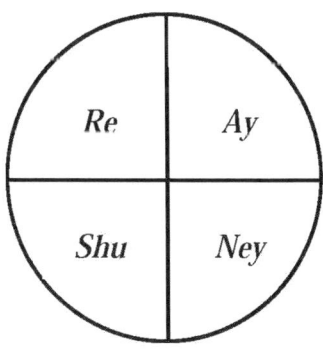

Examples of manifested forms of these elements are:

**Re:** fire, sun/sunlight, gold metal, cosmic spiritual light *(amun)*, south

**Ay:** Earth *(geb)*, soil, wood, flesh, west

**Shu:** air, gases, sound, sky *(nut)*, journeys/travel, east

**Ney:** water and water bodies *(net)*, ice, blood, emotions, flood *(nun)*, north

These elementals are associated with the four sacred cardinal points of south, west, east, and north. These four cardinal points describe universal direction rather than earthly direction. They are the directions from which the elementals first arose and moved forward to fill our universe. The four sacred elementals are considered to have an everlasting spiritual consciousness, but they have no single or final physical manifestation. The cosmic essence that constitutes Re, Ay, Shu, and Ney is eternal, but its manifestations are multitudinous and change with universal evolution.

The four sacred elementals are known collectively as *phah*. More specifically, phah is a person or group's connection to nature and the elements. Nature, in this instance, means all life-forms and substances that arise naturally through the evolution of the four sacred elementals. The initiates are taught that they are one and the same with phah; they can never truly separate themselves physically or spiritually from the elementals. The students are also taught and encouraged to strengthen their connection to, and understanding of, nature and elemental powers. The Earth's

*The Sacred Elementals and the Alchemy of Spirit* 41

natural environment and life-forms provide deep insight into the true nature of human beings. By understanding nature, the initiates begin to understand themselves.

This connection to phah is one of the four foundations of the spiritual ascension pyramid, as explained in chapter 2. Not only must initiates maintain a balance of the four elements within their own being, they must also attain a continual external connection to phah in its totality (as part of Ra-Harakhty).

Maintaining a balance of the four elements means paying equal attention to all aspects of life, and integrating the manifested forms of Re, Ay, Shu, and Ney into daily living—when and as they are required. For example: drinking water when one is thirsty; seeking a relationship when one is lonely; sitting in the sun when one is drained; or listening to music when one is agitated. This sounds easy, but it is not. In order to balance the phah, the initiate must know what needs to be done at what time and to what degree. This requires extraordinary intuition. In the distracting chaos of earthly life, few achieve a healthy and lasting phah. Because phah is a requirement for spiritual enlightenment, or illumination, those who achieve phah (in tandem with a balanced ka, ra, and ptah) are classified as masters or pharas.

A continued imbalance of any of the four elements within a person or society will lead to a slowing in evolution or even to a complete collapse of growth. For example, Re is the element connected with aggression, assertiveness, and masculinity. There have been societies on Earth whose Re grew too large at the expense of Ay, Shu, and Ney. As a consequence, world consciousness—which is intrinsically part of the elemental consciousness—might have sent a flood to counteract the situation. A flood, or nun, is of the Ney element, which is in the opposing quadrant to Re and is therefore the ideal element to neutralize too much Re.

The river Negeb, which flows through our land and supports all life, is a combination of the Ney and Ay elements. The Negeb is where sacred waters meet sacred land to form a river, which we believe has its own consciousness and reason for existence. The deep inhalations and exhalations of the Negeb form the tides, and every year this great river allows the flooding, or nun, at the autumnal equinox. The annual flooding also reminds us of our ancestors who were brought to Egypt along the Negeb course after the global Atlantian flood.

◟

The sacred elementals are the foundation of all alchemical processes—both physical and spiritual—throughout the universe. One of the primary objectives of the Mysterie Schools is the transformation of human existence via alchemy. Alchemy, in this instance, can be described as the application of energetic practices to raise and balance the consciousness of human beings. Spiritual alchemy, as applied within our school system, aims to convert energetic vibrations at a cellular level into the Golden Ray, which is an energy wave that carries particles vibrating at the highest frequencies. The Golden Ray is the ultimate alchemical state, which we require our students to reach, and it corresponds to the top of the universal pyramid in consciousness terms. (See chapter 8 for a further description of the Golden Ray.)

Attaining the Golden Ray entails transforming the base elements—of which human beings are constituted—into elements of a superior and more resilient quality. Let us refer to the list of elements above that derive from the sacred elementals.

The emotion of anger and angelic light both belong to the elemental group of Re. human beings are able to experience anger, but they are equally able to experience angelic light within their beings. The individual chooses which manifestation of Re to experience at a particular moment in time. You may say, "I have no choice over my emotions" or "I cannot help what I feel," but we say that you can. Choosing to experience the vibration of angelic light over an emotion like anger naturally raises the vibration of the body's cells towards the Golden Ray. The vibratory energy of angelic light is superior to that of anger in alchemical terms. Angelic light is a more resilient and purer energy.

As the students progress through the school system, an alchemical change occurs within their energetic bodies as they attune gradually with a heightened elemental state. This conditioning towards the highest manifestations of Re, Ay, Shu, and Ney is also referred to as the spiritual alchemical process of The Golden Ray. The Golden Ray can be described as an advanced state of consciousness that contains the highest universal energetic vibrations. The beings of the Angelic Realm exist continuously within The Golden Ray. It is a state to which we urge our students to aspire, but it cannot be explained—only experienced. The Golden Ray is the dimension in which eternal peace exists.

Eternal peace cannot be brought down to the conditions of the Earth—rather, human beings need to ascend energetically via an alchemical transformation into The Golden Ray—an existence in which peace can be achieved.

# 5
# Hieroglyphs and the Alphabet

Within our society we use a dual alphabetical system—two alphabets that can be used together or separately.

The original alphabet is the high-alphabet, sometimes called the feeling-alphabet or the language of the stars. It consists of a series of hieroglyphs that communicate universal concepts only, and no direct word translation can be made from them in a literary sense. Examples of the high-alphabet are the omnipotent concepts of love, truth, and everlasting life. In a sense, this primordial alphabet is not really an alphabet at all because it attempts to communicate certain ideas rather than literal meanings.

The second alphabet is the common alphabet (also called the literary alphabet), which can more directly be converted into other languages. The common alphabet is used in everyday proceedings, such as correspondence, business, accounting, record- and time-keeping.

The visual difference between the two alphabets relates to the size, layout, and surface of the text. The high-alphabet glyphs are larger, clearer, and more intermittent in their layout; they are not used unnecessarily. They only appear on the stonemasonry and possessions of the Mysterie Schools, such as ancient buildings and temples, meditation caskets, and sacred jewelry. Good examples are those that decorate the walls of temples or the passage chambers and alcoves of the meditation retreats. These are bold, colorful, and often self-explanatory images. The glyphs for the high-alphabet are also limited in number and contain an eternal, universal meaning while the glyphs of the common alphabet continue to expand with societal evolution.

The common alphabet is reserved for daily administration and communication. Counting, maintaining agricultural records, corresponding, and other day-to-day tasks use the words or letters of the common alphabet. This alphabet is written in narrow columns or rows, usually on papyrus paper. We teach the common alphabet with the understanding that it is transient, pertaining to a particular time and place. Many glyphs—such as the feather, basket, and quail chick—are used in both the common and high-alphabets. However, where the high-alphabet uses these images to convey a general meaning that transcends language, the common alphabet assigns a sound (or a letter/letters) to the symbol.

A selection of high-alphabet glyphs appears in chapter 14.

In our society, it is considered a great skill to be able to read and write, and this ability is often restricted to the students of the Mysteries. A large part of the Egyptian society outside of the Mysterie Schools is illiterate. This is unfortunate, since it was never our intention to maintain a monopoly on literacy, but we cannot take responsibility for society at large. In the temples of the Mysterie Schools, we teach both versions of our written communication, the high-alphabet and the common alphabet. However, although the common alphabet is taught and used outside of our school system, the high-alphabet is the exclusive reserve of the schools. It is only understood, and applied, by initiates of the Mysteries—specifically those who have passed a certain level. The high-alphabet is exclusively facilitated, cultivated, and communicated through our school system; external society is not privy to its meanings and secrets. As priests and high-priests of the Mysterie Schools, we are considered sacred keepers of the high-alphabet and are required in this role to teach this universal alphabet to initiates of a certain level only.

It is not possible for initiates to fully understand (or resonate with) the meanings of the feeling glyphs unless they are wholly a part of the spiritual ascension process that the schools aim to achieve. Therefore, as the students move higher in their degrees of learning, the high-alphabet glyphs take on evermore meaning and eventually transcend the two-dimensional imprint that they have been given in physical reality. For this reason, the high-alphabet—whilst easy to comprehend intellectually—is metaphysically profound to grasp and requires much concentrated study. The high-alphabet is more like a living commitment to the sacred mystical life that we strive to facilitate for the students. The glyphs of the high-alphabet are universal concepts and not just particular to human life on Earth. The high-alphabet is sacred, and its secrets are only revealed to the devoted students of mysticism—those initiates who reach Level 5.

▼

To be a scribe in our society is a very prestigious profession. The qualified scribes who serve those in authority outside of our temples are all schooled in the Mysteries. Thoth—the god of written truth—watches over them and guides them in their work that they might correctly capture all recorded truth. (See Thoth, chapter 12.)

We place so much emphasis on sacred writing because it is one of the few things that is able, if used correctly, to transcend place and time. To vandalize or incorrectly use our high-alphabet text is considered heretical in the extreme.

Within the high-alphabet there are seven sacred concepts that are part of the universal laws that govern all life and therefore receive honor. This enhancement is provided by an ovoculum, which is a knotted circlet glyph, and is explained in chapter 14. The ovoculum holds the meaning of the glyph concept within a sacred space since these concepts are transcendental to this world and applicable to all universal life in totality.

These seven concepts are: Love, Light, Truth, Prayer, Peace, Faith, and Sound. The ovocula for these seven concepts may be found in chapter 15, along with descriptions and explanations.

The accurate interpretation of the high-alphabet and the seven sacred concepts requires years of training—and more likely many lifetimes. While the seven sacred concepts, as well as the high-alphabet, are simple to understand in intellectual terms, supreme mastery is required to understand them on the emotional and spiritual levels. When a child is born, its mother can soon teach it the meaning of the word *love*. Within a few years, the child may have developed its own understanding of what love means and how love is communicated by its family and others around it. However, as that child grows within the turbulent world, the meaning of love is likely to change, taking on all sorts of new meanings and conditions. Quite often, the individual will reject love at some time in their life, temporarily, or even permanently.

One of the aims of the Mysterie Schools is to educate and guide students through earthly life by facilitating their understanding and application of the seven sacred concepts of universal life. So in our example, the objective would be for the individual to understand what unconditional love means on a universal level and to be able to apply it consistently within their life. It is easy enough for a person to perceive the idea of love, but to practice love, to communicate love, to give and receive love, unconditionally—in other words, to *become* love—is the ultimate goal. When a person is vibrating in the octave of love, they truly understand the ovocula of that particular concept and so have translated the glyphs on an energetic level. Understanding the high-alphabet involves not an interpretation of the mind but an interpretation of the soul.

Please see the glyph chapters 14-16, which will be continually referenced throughout the book.

Our initiates take much time and practice to master the art of reading and writing the high-alphabet. We have stonemasonry design tools and templates to create the glyphs. These were a gift brought by our ancestors from Atlantis, who had the foresight to know that we would need to recreate our society on another continent.

# 6
# Temples of the Skies

The Mysterie Schools are spread amongst the series of temples that line the Negeb river. The Negeb was known in our time as the River of Stars, since it grew to reflect the heavenly sweep of the great stellar vulture directly above; the temples and sacred sites along the river mirrored certain positions of the fixed stars. Most of the temples were built prior to 10,000 BCE—before our ancestors arrived in the land you know as Egypt. Some of the temples were built later, but all of the original buildings in use by the Mysterie Schools were complete by 8,500 BCE. Intergalactic beings built most of our temples, as well as the pyramids, although we did add to them over time—mostly using the advanced architectural and stonemasonry tools brought by our ancestors from Atlantis.

The pylons and hypostyle halls of the temples were originally for landing spacecraft. The pylons are the wall-like structures at the front of the temples, and the hypostyle halls often follow from the pylons. The halls are cavernous spaces interspersed with enormous pillars that once supported roofs for landing craft. Ground-level teleport chambers led off from below the landing area or were positioned somewhere close to the front of the buildings. Later, once the intergalactic beings had removed their influence from Earth (post 8,500 BCE), the landing stations were extended more adequately into temples. The temples were laid out in a replica of the holy temple of Akasha—also symbolic of the soul's journey towards inner mastery.

The initiates are required, as in boarding-school, to live at one of the temples during their tuition. There are terms of study, between which the initiates may return home, or they may remain at the schools for their own personal learning time. Many of the students are housed at the head-temple of Karnak in Thebes (Luxor). Karnak means *place of healing* (making the ka whole). Our major ceremonies are held at the adjacent temple that is now called the Luxor temple. Both temples may be referred to as centers of light. (See Amun-Ra in chapter 12.) In fact, any building or temple proclaiming an allegiance to Amun refers to the presence of light, specifically cosmic spiritual light.

Students may be taught at the other temples along the Negeb, but several years of each initiate's training must be done at Karnak because it is the epicenter of the Mysteries. Certain temples, such as the Philae, or Temple of Love, are reserved for special ceremonies or for certain advanced levels of learning that require a higher degree of removal from society.

Within the Mysteries, the study of sacred geometry takes up almost a full year of accumulated learning. We cannot go into the mystical, cosmological aspects of sacred geometry—or what we call *sodarlory* (pronounced so-daa-lor-I)—within this text, but we would like to bring a few points to your attention.

The temples were not built randomly along the banks of the river Negeb. We believe that the river mirrors the sweep of stars across the wings of the heavenly Sky Vulture, which is our interpretation of your Milky Way. (See Nekhabet/Sky Vulture in chapter 12.). The planet Earth is like an energetic pin cushion. The places on Earth that reflect certain stars, planets, and constellations acquire the intense, magnetic energy of these heavenly bodies. What appears above is reflected below. Whether there is a natural or human-made structure in that geographical place or not, the energies remain intense at that point on the Earth's surface.

These places of intense celestial energy are similar to energetic portals. At these locations, which we call *sedjes* (pronounced *sedges* and meaning *reflectors*), the veil between the physical world and the ethereal world is much thinner. It is easier to get in touch with cosmological energies and attune with all-that-is at the sedjes. Our temples, and the great pyramids, are built upon the sedjes and the sedj-line, which is the sacred invisible cord that connects the sedjes along the Negeb. The positioning of these sacred temples and monuments ensures that they receive the highest possible energetic influence from the heavens, so that, within them, we may do our best spiritual work.

The temples are also aligned with the positions of the sun at the equinoxes and solstices. For example, Karnak faces the setting sun at the summer solstice—corresponding to the time that it was built. Since the sundisc is a manifested form of our overall god-energy, or Sun God, we like to continually pay homage to the energy of the sun. (See chapter 12, introduction.) The sunlight at the four cardinal points of the year often floods the inner sanctum of the temples.

▼

We would like to explain our understanding of the term *stars*. What you call stars we call light-bodies. Although we will use the term *stars* as well throughout this text, stars usually refer to physical heavenly bodies that emit, or reflect, light. The difference in our terminology is that the stars you can observe from your planet Earth are not always physical. For example, the light-body Sirius is not a star at all but an intergalactic portal that continuously emits a tremendous amount of light. Similarly, the stars of Orion's belt and Aldebaran, which all fall upon the same celestial line, are not physical bodies either. This particular set of light-bodies are gateways to other worlds within our universe. There is no actual physical substance to these objects—they remain as light-emitters as long as the portal to which they lead remains open. If human beings could get close to these stars, they would see that no astral body exists at those places.

So, if an intergalactic being says that it is from Aldebaran, what it means is that it lives in the reality of Aldebaran, which is a planetary system accessed through the light-portal that we can see from the Earth as the "star" Aldebaran. The actual physical body or bodies that constitute Aldebaran are much, much further away than the visible light that the portal emits—in a distant part of the universe. The light-body space that can be seen from Earth as a star is merely the entrance to the Aldebaran world. The portal provides instant transference to the real Aldebaran, as well as to other places.

Similarly, the light-bodies of Orion's belt, as well as Sirius, are not astral bodies at all. For example, Sirius is the brightest and most active portal in the Earth's heavenly circumference. Sirius is a busy highway of beings entering and exiting the Earth's immediate celestial system.

The name *Osiris* is a combination of the portal names of Orion and Sirius (see Osiris in chapter 12). The southern shaft of our great pyramid is aligned with Orion's belt; the northern shaft is aligned with Thuban, the ancient pole star of the Dragon constellation. Although the Earth's pole star is technically an impermanent point, Thuban is the point to which the Earth's magnetic north aligns repeatedly over the ages. Thuban is like point zero—or the equilibrium point of a pendulum—through which the planet's alignment will never cease to pass. Thuban is also circumpolar (never-setting) and so served as a celestial navigator during our time.

Thuban is also not a real, physical astral body; like Aldebaran or Sirius, it is a light-body established temporarily (in universal terms) to support the planet Earth. A profound quantity of celestial light may be aimed at the planet Earth from the Thuban portal, and shone, like a laser, into the Earth's energy grid. This method of light infusion has been used several times during planet Earth's history to raise its energetic vibration and improve its constitution. However, the laser has not been used for Earth in a while. A planet naturally adopts the state of its inhabitants; human beings are now responsible for achieving and maintaining the energetic state of their own planet. Before humans existed, however, and at times when there wasn't much conscious life on the Earth, universal forces needed to occasionally intervene with light injections to stabilize the planet.

In summary, the alignment of the great pyramid with the pole star ensured that the gigantic pyramid absorbed as much of the light frequencies as possible, even when the portal was inactive. The shaft that runs from the meditation chamber at the center of the great pyramid is both a channel for the celestial Thuban light and a cosmic torch for the initiate who is experiencing trans-meditation within the structure. The initiates always require these light-bodies to find their way through the heavens and back to their physical bodies. The Orion shaft has a similar effect.

Chapter 9 explains trans-meditation and how the light-body portals are used by the initiates in their astral journeys.

The three great pyramids of our land, Iyrgr, are positioned to mirror the light-bodies of Orion's belt. As we have explained, this ensures that the energetic vibration of these structures is maximized. Orion's belt is part of the Orion constellation and is constituted of three light-bodies. The northern-most star of the belt, Mintaka, falls upon the celestial equator. The other two stars, Alnilam and Alnitak, form a celestial line that meets with the portal Sirius to the south and Aldebaran to the north. In these instances, we are referring to universal directions.

The three light-bodies of Orion's belt are the main portals through which universal energies and beings have been active during the existence of Earth. Although we are not going to expand upon the Earth creation within this book, it is important to state that Earth and the human race are an experiment in polarities (dual energies). The Earth, and its life-forms, are no more an experiment than is the rest of our universe; it is just that Earth is the most recent of the celestial experiments and has been receiving a lot of attention, particularly over the last million Earth years.

The universal friends of the Earth and the human race have used the Orion (and Sirius) portals since the experiment began. The intensely positive energy that is concentrated within these portals acts like acupuncture on the planet; the cosmic light shafts extend down and into the physical body of the Earth herself.

# Temples of the Skies

Placing the three great pyramids at these points was advantageous, to say the least. It also ensured that the land of Iyrgr was consecrated as holy. Although the theories behind the construction of the pyramids and temples are no longer entirely applicable in the modern age, it is good that the physical structures remain at those geographical points, mainly to honor and act as a reminder of why they were originally constructed.

In chapter 12 we explain that Osiris means *service to life,* and therefore it is apt that the name derives from the Orion and Sirius portals through which the greatest universal help arrived for the Earth planet. Those energies and entities that passed into the Earth's system through these portals did so in an act of service to life and absolute love of their fellow life-forms.

▼

What may be confusing to you is that the position of the Earth in the universe has changed over the millennia since our ancestors came from Atlantis. Intergalactic beings were preparing the temples and pyramids prior to the fall of Atlantis, which sank in approximately 10,000 BCE. Therefore, many of the celestial, solar, and lunar alignments of our stone structures were created for conditions as they existed before the fall of Atlantis—even as far back as 12,000 BCE. The stone structures were designed to withstand flood and were submerged below the Atlantian floodwaters for almost a year. The waters receded quickly, and the structures were unharmed.

You will notice that no concrete is used in our buildings. This is because the blocks are precisely chiseled to fit together and create a vacuum. In fact, the pressure from the floodwaters would have reinforced the adhesive relationships of the blocks. Sound was the tool used to cut, lift, and arrange the blocks of the temples and pyramids. The sound process is explained further in chapters 8 and 9.

# 7
# Our Colorful Universe

L ight is a fundamental concept of universal life and is represented by the following glyph.

**This ovoculum of our high-alphabet means Light.**

All seven colors of the physical light spectrum are represented in this glyph—specifically the visible light of the electromagnetic wave continuum. The colors are red, orange, yellow, green, blue, indigo, and violet (see chapter 15 for the Light ovoculum). Because human vision is trichromatic, all of these colors are a result of combinations of the three primary colors of light—red, green, and blue. In other words, the human eye can only interpret variations of these seven colors, which are in essence combinations of the three basic primary colors.

Seven colors of the rainbow are manifested within each human being through the seven primary chakras. These are invisible energy vortices, which spin like wheels at various points in a straight line between the tail and crown of each person. The seven energy chakras of the physical body vibrate at the frequencies akin to the color that they represent. For example, the first, or base, chakra is red. This energy vortex vibrates within the lowest electromagnetic energy frequency on the light spectrum and has the longest wavelength. The heart, or fourth, chakra resonates with the color green, having a wavelength and frequency approximately in the middle of the visible light spectrum. The seventh, or crown, chakra is the most interesting of all. In a healthy person, it will vibrate at the highest frequency with the shortest wavelength in accordance with deep purple—or violet. If sufficiently developed, the violet chakra will spin widely enough to include the colors of the other six chakras, thereby forming a white orb around the deep violet crown chakra.

The chakra system begins at the base of the trunk of the human body and ends right at the top of the head. The invisible line upon which the chakras vibrate is called the auratic colombine. The auratic colombine serves as a dual channel for the internal energies that enliven the human body—the chakras—as well as for migrating energies brought into the body, and leaving the body, on an ongoing basis.

The chakra system is unique to each human being; upon death, the energy centers remain as an imprint with the ascending soul that leaves the body. Therefore, the chakra system is linked to the physical body within human manifestation but is more accurately a part of the spiritual body of human beings.

Life on Earth usually erodes the state of the chakras; planetary conditions have not yet evolved sufficiently to support permanent healthy energy systems. Therefore, the initiates are taught a multitude of methods to increase and maintain the health of their chakras. These methods include elemental balancing (see chapter 4); physical exercises and yoga; breathing techniques; sound, energy, and light therapies; and mystic meditation.

▼

We assume that you already know a good deal about the chakra system, and so we will not go into too much further detail on the specific centers. However, we would like to mention a bit more about the auratic colombine. This channel is so called because it allows the movement of energy between the body and the environments outside of the body. This can refer to immediate environments in direct contact with the physical body and also to environments in the most distant corners of the universe. Since everything in creation is connected indirectly on a physical level and directly on the emotional, spiritual, and mental levels, there is little separating each individual from every other part of life.

From our perspective as ascended beings, we see that everything is connected to everything else, simply by being part of an evolving whole. Every living thing is part of, and therefore affected by, the entire universe in which we exist. As an analogy, even a tiny ant on Earth is influenced by planetary shifts and changes—whether or not it is aware that it is part of an enormous planet. And so, all humans alive on planet Earth are affected by universal changes—whether or not they know or accept that they are part of a complex system. You cannot separate yourself from any part of life in the multidimensional universe in which you exist as a spiritual and physical being.

In terms of the physical aspect of life, the universal connection is mostly an indirect one. We can understand that a nuclear waste dump exists on the same planet as ourselves, but we can choose to distance ourselves physically from that site. Emotionally, spiritually, and mentally, our connections to all of life are far more direct. This is because everything derives from one source of creation: all-that-is. From where we gaze down upon your planet, we see the human race as operating with a single mind, and as a single spiritual creature, with common emotions. This does not mean that you are all existing simultaneously at the same levels of mental, spiritual, and emotional evolution; rather, none of you can ever be completely separated from the whole. This whole may refer to your planet, the human race, or the universe at large.

We also assume that you will already have a good idea of the connection between all things, and so we would like to explain the role of the auratic colombine further in this respect. The auratic colombine, while acting as a channel for transient energies, also performs a filtering function. The colombine is a column that allows energy to enter and exit the human system, but it is also a defense mechanism against unwanted energies. Even though we are all connected, we have the power to choose which energies we allow to influence our system and which we don't.

The auratic colombine acts as a neutral zone that can accommodate energies of all types for a while—long enough for us to choose whether they will serve us or not. The colombine is like an interstate highway that carries vehicles of all types from one place to another. It is our choice as individuals to allow certain energies to turn off that highway and join our energy system. The colombine does not have the physical limit of length and can be extended into any part of the universe at will. Think of it as an energetic tube of expanding and contracting light—the light particles may travel as far as they like in any direction. The auratic colombine thus serves as our connection to all of life and is the ethereal part of us that remains eternally bound to all-that-is.

The initiates of the Mysteries are taught methods to sensitize themselves acutely to energy vibrations, both in their immediate vicinity and into the broader universe. As a result, they are able to use higher-states of consciousness to feel energies at great distances that come into contact with their individual auratic colombines. The initiates use auratic sensing as one method to develop their psychic faculties. If they sense bad energies, they are able to either avoid or prepare to face the various conditions that bring the unwanted energy. Alternatively, the students are taught to extend their colombines deep into space as well as into the heart of mother Earth, drawing on the superb energies that are available to everybody at all times.

The auratic colombine, like many things, goes by a number of other names; it really doesn't matter what we call it. What is important is that it serves as a vital channel that provides you with an opportunity to balance your own energy systems and find harmony with universal forces.

Returning to color: the auratic colombine is so called partly because it is the source of the human aura. The aura can be described in many ways, but it is simply the energetic snapshot of a body or entity at a point in time. The aura can be seen as a series of colors—or pattern of colors. The colors produced by the chakra centers reflect, and are blended within, the auratic colombine. Just as the energy system of an individual is subtly changing in accordance with the ever-present, so the colors moving through the colombine are changing at every moment in time. However, the energy pattern produced in the colombine is relatively consistent from one moment to the next because energy changes usually happen gradually—except in certain instances like trauma or accident.

Certain psychic faculties allow some individuals to see the aura around a human body, but it is invisible to most people. However, the inability of most people to physically observe the aura does not stop color being used to heal the human body via the chakra system. Vibrations of color sensed within the auratic colombine can energize the chakra system into better states of health, thereby improving the overall auratic imprint. It is important to get the auratic imprint into an optimal condition and maintain that auratic color pattern, because this pattern travels with the ascending soul when it makes the transition from physical life. The auratic imprint is part of the spiritual body of human beings, and it will move with them from lifetime to lifetime.

This is why our Mysterie Schools place so much emphasis on healing and spiritual mastery; attaining higher-states of spiritual health and consciousness is not particular to an individual lifetime but rather to an individual soul.

Color therapy for healing is used extensively throughout the schools—mostly in the form of colored light, crystals, and the creative visual arts. Color therapy is often applied in tandem with sound therapy. Both color and sound therapy are part of our healing arts; particular colors and sounds are inseparable vibrations of the same energetic frequency. This is discussed in the following chapter.

You will notice that many of our glyphs and ornaments contain the primary colors red, green, and blue; specifically the repeating pattern of blue, red, blue, green, blue, red, blue, green. We have explained that these are the three primary colors of the visible light spectrum from which all other color is derived. The reason the schools place so much emphasis on color and light is that light produces all life. On a more mundane or scientific level, the light from the sun is the source of energy for all life on Earth. On a spiritual level, everything that exists on Earth and in the universe is composed of cosmic light. Cosmic light includes particle waves from the entire electromagnetic spectrum (from radio to gamma rays, and beyond to infinity)—not just the thin sliver of visible light that we know as the rainbow.

Within the schools however, we consider the physical light spectrum, and specifically the three primary colors, as critical to spiritual life. This is because it is the visible color band that gives meaning to three-dimensional life, particularly in the human body on planet Earth. Light only exists on your planet because of the rays of the sun. Objects reflect the sun's light during daylight hours. The sun's light contains all colors of the visible light spectrum and so appears white. Objects will absorb all of the light waves from the sun except those of their own particular color, which they will reflect. Human beings see objects as various colors (if you have been graced with the gift of clear sight).

However, you are not seeing the actual object but the light that reflects off that object. No matter how solid your surroundings appear, your faculty of sight is completely reliant on the full light spectrum provided by the sun. Your physical surroundings remain an illusion, since you are relying on the information brought to you by light waves to interpret our world. Of course, there are other faculties like touch and hearing that add to the overall illusion, but these faculties are quite removed from the essence of who you are as a spiritual being and are therefore not wholly reliable. As a human being, you are continually depending on indirect messages through your senses to confirm who and what you are and what your moment-to-moment reality is.

Through the auratic colombine you get the truest sense of things around you. The colombine, as explained, is a non-dimensional spiritual part of yourself and therefore not reliant on the various senses of the physical human body to define itself. It forms the basis of what you might understand as extrasensory perception and is the reason why some blind people can become expert navigators without sight.

We advocate to our students that it is vital to develop and use the power of the auratic colombine to its highest potential. Simultaneously, we celebrate the three-dimensional human form. The human eye is part of a body that exists in a material world on a physical plane of reality. The human eye can only see the primary colors of light: blue, red, and green. All other colors of the visible spectrum are manufactured within the eye and understood by the brain—but the human eye never actually sees them. Because all colors of light are ultimately a combination of the three primary colors, the eye can understand color via the frequencies of light that enter it without necessarily seeing the colors. The various colors of the rainbow are subsequently constructed using the primary color frequencies as a base-palette.

We believe that the physical limitations of the eye in seeing color are symbolic of the limitations a human being experiences in life on Earth. After all, humans are first and foremost spiritual beings who incarnate in physical bodies to develop their souls. It is not easy to master a three-dimensional reality in a physical body when the objective is a spiritual one—but it is possible. The manner in which the human mind enables a person to experience all colors of the rainbow, when he actually hasn't seen those colors in reality, is symbolic of the spiritual heights a person can achieve in life on Earth. This is analogous to our belief in the human ability to reach its highest spiritual potential, whether or not individuals develop the faculties to evolve beyond their physical limitations. All and any limits of the three-dimensional human body or environment are merely illusions. The human body is merely a vessel for spiritual work, and the planet Earth a sacred location that has been provided as a gift towards this end.

Therefore, the schools endlessly celebrate the human ability to see the three primary colors; most creatures on Earth cannot see color at all. Blue is the primary color with the shortest wavelength but the highest frequency, and it is therefore the primary color that vibrates at the highest rate. Blue is particularly celebrated because it is the most spiritually ascended primary color that the eye can actually see. Working through the chakra system from red to violet, blue is the color of the fifth, or throat, chakra and therefore the color out of the three primaries closest to the most advanced, and spiritually connected, crown chakra of violet/white. The blue, or fifth, level also corresponds with the rate at which the planet Earth naturally vibrates at her highest potential; and towards which she is in a current state of ascension.

⏷

Although we teach that the human eye can see only the three primary colors, there is no limit to the light that individuals can embody via their chakra systems and auratic colombines. This is further evidence that humans are able to rise above the limitations of the physical body, since they can reflect all colors of the multicolored universe on a metaphysical level. It is really quite beautiful.

In chapter 2 we discussed how levels of consciousness rise towards enlightenment—the top of the pyramid. Enlightenment is so called because it is a measure of the amount of light a body can hold. The more spiritually advanced individuals become, the more light their physical bodies are able to accommodate. This not only refers to the quantity of light but more specifically to the frequency of that light. The higher on the color rainbow we progress, and the higher the vibration of a particular color, the more advanced that light is considered spiritually. However, the more that light vibrates, the more a body must be transformed to facilitate this light. Enlightenment is an alchemical process. The cells of the body need to learn how to embody higher frequencies of light through the continued application of spiritually conscious practices of ever-increasing difficulty. Enlightenment is an evolutionary process that becomes exponentially more challenging to master.

The entire school system is designed to guide the initiates

towards raising their cellular frequency in accordance with increased illumination. We apply a multitude of practices and techniques to enable the students to become more conscious and reach enlightenment—or at least to reach their highest potential consciousness. It is important to note that the level of consciousness cannot be faked by an individual, nor can the ascension process be rushed. As mentioned, it is an alchemical process that occurs in every cell of the human body, and every natural procedure requires time as a key ingredient to a successful result. Although we have a multitude of techniques to quickly—and almost artificially—raise the energetic vibration of people, these are used cautiously within a particular context and only when appropriate. Raising human energetic states is part of our healing arts, whose techniques are applied in tandem with an individual's ascension up the energy spiral.

Eventually, the auratic colombine will resonate with the overall base frequency of an individual, and this vibration will permeate through every cell of the body. The base frequency is the lowest, or default, rate at which an individual vibrates. They might waver around this frequency, and sometimes exceed it, but it will be the frequency to which their body will return while in a normal state of awareness. We have measurement methods and tools to test at what base level an individual is resonating. As mentioned in previous chapters, these are objective testing methods and can be influenced neither by the initiate nor the one doing the testing.

The ultimate frequency that we aim for corresponds to the color white. Upon full enlightenment, the chakra centers of an individual's energy system should be vibrating at the optimal frequencies associated with the seven colors of the rainbow. When blended within the auratic colombine, the resultant color is a brilliant white. As mentioned before, illumination is a supreme goal to reach and it is neither quick nor easy to attain this state of being. We personally, as priests and priestesses, have only experienced a small percentage of cases where initiates have reached this level. We anticipate that as your planet shifts into the new dimension, which it is doing now, more and more Earth natives will attain enlightenment.

Many of our hieroglyphics and other decorations use the primary colors. The color pattern frequently seen on our art is blue, red, blue, green, blue, red, blue. The significance of the color blue has been explained above, and it is the color that forms the buffer between the red and green primaries. This alternating color pattern produces all the colors of the rainbow in the correct order when applied to white light.

Let us imagine a color wheel divided into the three primary colors of light: red, green, and blue. Combining red with green forms shades of orange/yellow; red with blue creates shades of violet/indigo; green with blue produces variations of green/blue. Therefore, within this color wheel, all colors of the rainbow are represented. The color wheel is like a turning dial, at the center of which, the combination of the seven colors of the rainbow will create white light.

# Our Colorful Universe

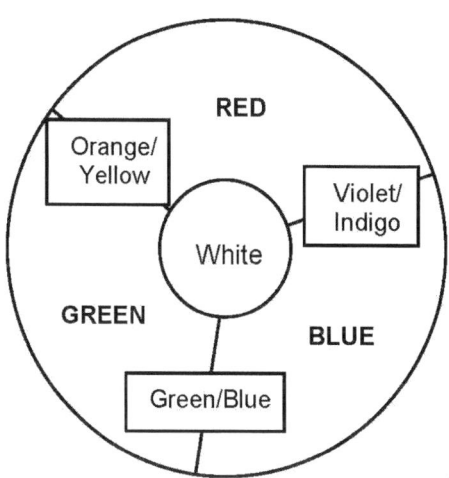

Every color possibility in the wheel of light exists as a ratio of the three primary colors. Changing the ratio of the primaries changes the resultant colored light. This is unlike the mixing of paints in a palette where the colors are being added one of top of another. The addition of a primary color in light refers to increasing its ratio in proportion to the other two primaries. In the diagram below, this is why green plus blue can produce yellow, because we are not adding green to blue, but rather increasing the proportion of blue within an existing red, green, blue ratio to create yellow.

Red + BLUE = Violet
Violet + RED = Indigo
Indigo + BLUE = Blue
Blue + GREEN = Green
Green + BLUE = Yellow
Yellow + RED = Orange
Orange + BLUE = Red

The alternating pattern of primary light used in the example above acts like a crystal prism, splitting white light into a full rainbow. In three dimensions, the white light will form a rainbow pyramid.

# 8
# Sacred Sounds and the Seven Rays

Sound has been used within our schools as a healing tool for thousands of years. Sacred sound instruments were brought from the Atlantis continent by our ancestors. When the ancestors arrived in the land of Egypt, the three great pyramids and many of the temples had already been built by intergalactic beings. Far to the south, two sound chambers had been carved out of dome mountains at the place that is now called Abu Simbel.

We refer to this sacred place of sound healing as the Ramasseum (pronounced Ra-ma-see-im), which means *place of the still sounding waters* in an ancient dialect.

This is an ovoculum of our high-alphabet which means *Sound*. See chapter 15 for a full explanation.

    There are various ways in which we use sound to heal and to raise the energy vibration of the initiates. Mostly, we use voice intonations—specifically sacred vowel sounds—as well as tuning forks; giant wind chimes; musical instruments such as the sistrum or rattle, drums, harps, flutes, trumpets, and other sacred sound tools and instruments. We also use wooden resonator boxes to amplify sound, particularly for the tuning forks. The Ramasseum chambers are ideal for sound energy work because the vibrations are contained within a confined, holy structural space, and are intensified.

    Sacred sounds are linked to the seven colors of the rainbow—there being a frequency vibration for each of the seven colors corresponding to the seven sacred energy centers of the human body. The base chakra (sacred energy center) of the body appears red within the light spectrum because it is closest to Earth and vibrates with the lowest frequency. As we move up the chakra system, and ascend through the colors of the rainbow, the light frequency vibration becomes higher. Naturally, there are corresponding resonances to these various colors because the energy centers are constantly vibrating and therefore emitting a sound.

These sounds are undetectable to the human ear, especially with the humdrum noises of everyday life on Earth. We use various tools, including rods, to measure the vibration of an individual's energy centers and to assess whether they are in good working order. Also, we have tuning forks and instruments that emit the optimal sound frequencies at which the chakras should be vibrating. These optimal sound frequencies, if played intensely and for a sufficient time period, will naturally raise the vibrations of the chakra centers—returning individuals to a near perfect state of health.

The energy rods are also used to test a student's state of readiness during initiations. The rods are able to measure the overall base frequency at which an individual is vibrating, which gives us an indication of their consciousness level. Certain levels of learning require that an initiate be at a certain consciousness level; the initiate may not proceed until they have attained that level.

The tuning forks are used to balance the seven major energy centers. We use them, along with the energy rods, frequently within daily temple life. The initiates are also required to chant their vowel sounds each day. Vowel intonations created by the human voice produce healing resonances throughout the body. Sacred musical instruments are used in orchestra inside the chambers of the Ramasseum or at other gatherings.

The effect of any sounding, toning, or music within the Ramasseum is remarkable. The chambers of this complex contain and intensify sound, echoing it off the walls and filling every molecule of the chamber with glorious resonance. Each cell of the human beings within the chamber vibrates with the frequency of the sounds or music. The Ramasseum facilitates mass increases in energy consciousness and healing.

◆

Sound is universally recognized as the easiest way to physically influence objects at a distance. The blocks of the great pyramids and temples were cut and moved using sound harmonization—or vibrational chiseling. These methods are loosely referred to in your time as ultrasonic. Although we were not responsible for building the pyramids and most of the temples, our ancestors brought ancient sound-masonry tools from Atlantis, which we continued to use within the Mysterie Schools. These included quartz crystal tools, resonating ball tablets, and preconfigured masonry templates that we used to carve reliefs and hieroglyphs on surfaces, sculpt statues and obelisks, and for other aspects of stonework. The sound tools are the express property of the Mysterie Schools, and the skills required for the sacred masonry are passed down only through the school system.

◆

Sound is a universal language, and the frequencies of the chakras reflect the seven sacred cosmic sounds from which the entire universe was born. In reality, all languages are a series of sounds or intonations. The default universal language—and this may surprise you—is a refined form of your own English language. However, at the emotional-spiritual level, the default language is harmonic sound only. Just as a dual alphabetical system is used in our schools—of which one is a feeling form of communication (see

# Sacred Sounds and the Seven Rays

chapter 5)—so there is a universal form of communication that consists of sacred sounds only. This is because, as on your planet Earth, there are so many life-forms in our universe with so many varied forms of communication that sound is the quickest and easiest way to transmit universal messages.

Returning to the high- or feeling-alphabet, each one of the seven sacred ovocula has its own sound harmonic. (See ovocula, chapter 15.) These harmonics are generally a short series of sounds, or musical notes, which transmit the concept of the ovoculum energetically. In other words, the meaning of the ovocula can actually be felt through sound vibrations. In fact, for many of the ovocula, we have no actual Egyptian word for the sacred concept, and so when forced to express it verbally, we have to use sacred vowel sounds.

For instance, there is no word for *love*, and so we refer to the concept as oh-ma-ha, which derives from the sacred vowel sounds of the love feeling.

In further explanation, the Love ovoculum is transmitted by a trinity of sound—the musical notes *g, f,* and *d* in succession. These are hummed three times and then the piece is finished with a drawn-out *e* and *c*.

Humming:

g, f, d
g, f, d
g, f, d, e, c

The sacred vowel intonations are:

oh, ma, ha
oh, ma, ha
oh, ma, ha, ah, ha

If we were to add words, they would be:

We are one,
we are one,
we are one, mmm.

The animation symbol for the Love ovoculum is the goddess Isis crowned with a three-tiered xylophone. (See chapters 12 and 16 for a further explanation of Isis and the Isis animation symbols.) The three levels of the instrument represent the three musical notes g, f, and d in succession, including e and c.

Below is a side-profile of an African xylophone. The keys are slung down in an arc. The areas that include the relevant notes for love have been shaded. The primary three musical notes of *love*—g, f, and d—are underlined. The shading extends underneath the notes e and c too, since they are part of the overall intonation.

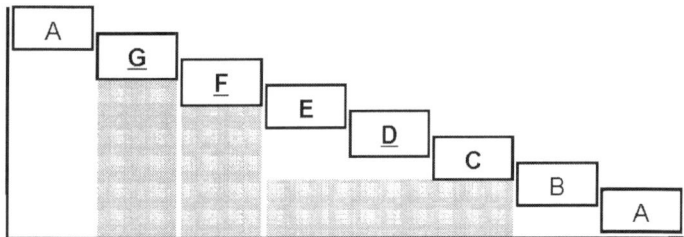

If the shaded blocks are removed and placed together, they form the foundation of the animation symbol of love/Isis. (In chapter 16, the animation symbol is extended in chorus as per the full intonation sequence.)

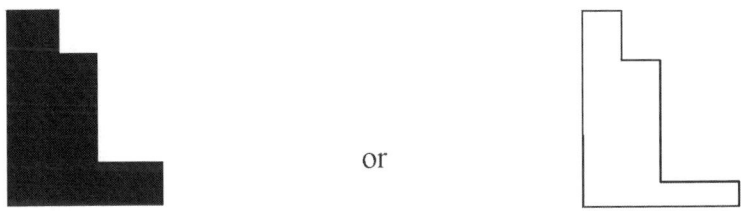

Another example is the ovoculum for Peace, which is a single drawn-out note c and corresponds to the vowel intonation of *om*.

Light is a little more complicated, since it includes the seven colors of the rainbow. The corresponding sound is an ascending scale of the seven musical notes from *a* to *g*, with the *g* held for emphasis.

a, b, c, d, e, f, ggg

The vowel sound equivalent for Light includes all of the seven sacred vowel sounds:

ra, ba, om, ha, ah, ma, oh (with the *oh* held for emphasis)

Most human voices cannot reach all of these seven notes easily, and so the intonations are either accompanied by, or replaced by, the singing bowl. The singing bowl is usually a metal or crystal bowl with a short thick wand that, when pressed and rotated around the inside of the bowl, produces clear, deep sounds. These sounds correspond to the seven musical notes and the seven vowel sounds. When the wand is drawn around the inside of the singing bowl, it produces a beautifully ascending scale of the seven sounds. It takes the initiates much practice to get all seven notes out of a single bowl, but it is important for them to produce their own sound because this increases the healing properties of the process.

The animation symbol for Light is the goddess Nephthys crowned with a singing bowl. (See chapters 12 and 16 for a further explanation on Nephthys and the Nephthys animation symbols.) In the image, the singing bowl usually stands on top of a vertical block. This stand acts like a resonation box and assists with the sound transmission.

▼

The initiates are required, amongst other chants, to hum or sing the intonations for the seven sacred ovocula every day. This not only balances their energy chakras but also connects them to the cosmos and aligns them with the higher celestial order.

You will have noticed many similarities between this chapter on sound and the previous chapters on color, energy, and consciousness. We believe that energy, color, and sound are indivisible manifestations of the same thing. There is a corresponding color and sound for every energetic level—or level of consciousness.

These three manifestations are the closest examples we have of the materialization of god or source-energy. Energy, color, and sound manifest most obviously in the human body along the auratic colombine, which facilitates the seven energy centers (chakras). Each chakra vibrates at a particular energetic rate, thus emitting a particular light frequency as well as the relevant sound vibration. The more conscious an individual, the more intensely the chakras, and particularly the higher chakras, will vibrate. All seven energy centers should be vibrating at their optimal frequencies. However, on Earth, different souls exist in different states of consciousness. The level of the highest, healthiest chakra is generally an indication of the overall energetic level of consciousness of an individual at a point in time. As explained in chapter 2, this reflects the current level of consciousness and does not necessarily indicate the full spiritual potential of the individual. We also refer to this as the base frequency (or default frequency) of an individual.

For example, if the first three chakras are fully activated and the chakras from the fourth level are weaker, then the overall energetic vibration of the person would be the third level (the solar-plexus chakra). If all seven of an individual's chakras are fully activated to their maximum potential, then the individual is existing in the highest state of consciousness possible. Anomalies can occur. For instance, a person might have evolved to the seventh level, but the third chakra could be in a weakened state at the time. In this case, the third chakra needs attention, but the weakness does not bring down the overall level of consciousness of the person, who has achieved the seventh already.

Of course, these manifestations within the human body are generally invisible. It is only through skilled psychic attunement and practical application of our healing tools and rods that the energy systems of humans can be objectively measured. There will come a time—not too far off—when scientific discovery on your planet will catch up with spiritual understanding, and instruments will be developed to measure the human energy system. Chakra, color, and sound readings and healings will become common practice again on the Earth.

⏾

We believe that everything in creation emits its own sound—from gigantic suns to the most minute grains of sand. The planets are unique in that they sing as they move in their orbits, as if issuing the sound of the giant singing bowl of the cosmos. True, each planet only emits its own particular tone, but it does so in unison with the other planets, which means the solar system plays a never-ending harmony that we know as the *music of the spheres*.

Your Earth vibrates naturally in the fifth dimension, or the musical note *e*, which corresponds to the color blue and the fifth energy chakra. We call your Earth the *blue planet* sometimes; not only does it appear blue by the presence of so much water on the surface but its aura resonates with a beautiful blue light that can be seen from a long distance away!

The seven chakras are not unique to the physical human being. These sacred energy centers repeat continually throughout life. The planet Earth has her own chakra system, and the solar system of which she is part is in essence like a celestial chakra system. On a grander scale, there is a universal chakra system, which is comprised of seven levels of consciousness that perpetually exist in all-that-is. These seven levels of consciousness manifest as The Seven Rays.

There is a sacred combination of numbers that we use, also known as 7:7:7. Specifically, this refers to 7 colors : 7 sounds : 7 energetic or chakra levels of consciousness. These are the quintessential, and three-dimensional, Seven Rays, also known as the Seven Harmonics (derived through the sound wave that accompanies the ray).

# Sacred Sounds and the Seven Rays

Almost all of the Mysterie Schools' teachings revolve around this trinity of seven, in which the three combinations are linked in an eternal dance of life.

In expansion:

Seven Colors

1. Red
2. Orange
3. Yellow
4. Green
5. Blue
6. Indigo
7. Violet

Seven Sounds

1. Ra
2. Ba
3. Om
4. Ha
5. Ah
6. Ma
7. Oh

Seven Energetic Levels or Chakra Centers

- Level 1
- Level 2

- Level 3
- Level 4
- Level 5
- Level 6
- Level 7

Below, the 7:7:7 trinity is represented on a ladder of light. The diagram attempts to show that light contains all sound, and sound contains all light, and that light and sound are part of the same energetic system. The hollow at the top of the ladder represents where all seven of the trinity combine to form absolute nothingness—or whiteness. This describes more than a color; it is the closest description we have of the Source or god-energy. As the whiteness intensifies, it becomes golden, and manifests the Golden Ray, which is symbolic of the highest octave of the 7:7:7 vibration. According to the laws of synergy, the Golden Ray is more powerful than the sum of the parts of all sound, color, and energy—it is consciousness itself. (The Golden Ray is also explained in chapter 4.)

# Sacred Sounds and the Seven Rays

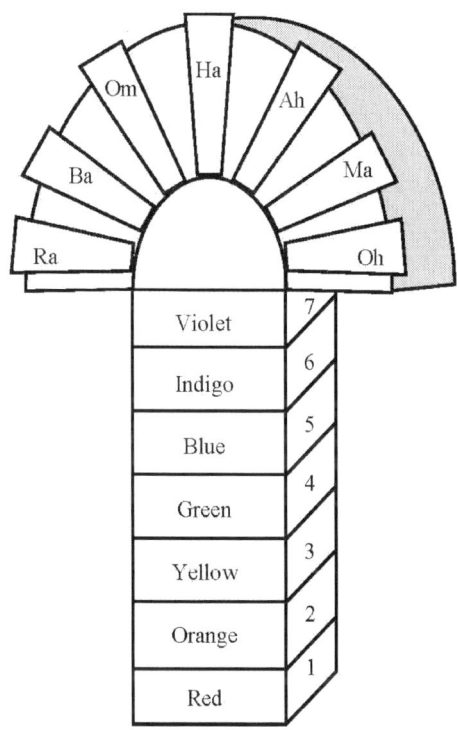

This image is similar to the pleated head-dress that some of our initiates wear (the Nemset, chapter 11). The arc at the top of the light-ladder is emulated in the head-dress by the alternating black (or blue) and gold ribs of the shroud. The pillar portion of the light-ladder is reflected as the folds of cloth that fall over the shoulders and back—also alternating black (or blue) and gold. The false beard, or chinstrap piece, is also similar in appearance to the pillar portion of the image above.

These two adornments are described in chapter 11, *Representations of Initiations Passed*. However, we would like to emphasize that wherever black/blue and gold alternating stripes appear in our art or clothing, it is a reference to the overcoming of duality. The black/blue bands represent the dark, or earthly, physical life; the gold bands represent the light—or heavenly spiritual life. human beings are dualistic creatures living in a bipolar world. Life on Earth is difficult. If humans can overcome the duality of their own natures, and in the world around them, then they have mastered the art of living on planet Earth.

Living within duality is primarily felt through the emotional structure of the human being. All emotions are a form of energy and so carry a sound. Therefore, all harmful emotions can be healed by sound, and pleasant emotions can be created by sound. We believe that sound is one of the primary methods of overcoming duality and negative human emotions. Sound harmonizes all the energies within physical (and non-physical) bodies. Peaceful sound vibrations provide a method for our energetic bodies to balance themselves; they are also a method to balance the conflicted emotional states that caused an energetic imbalance in the first place.

At the Ramasseum appear glyphs of the Sound ovoculum as a central figure in overcoming duality. For example, the Sound ovoculum is placed on the platform of the metaphorical heart-center (See chapter 14, Life Throne.) A pair of figures on either side tug in opposite directions at this heart-center—the dual nature of humankind or *Atum* (See chapter 12). Sound crowns the image, offering a method to harmonize the naturally bipolar nature of the human being.

# 9
# Trans-Meditation

Trans-meditation, also known as transcendental meditation, is a form of meditative practice that is used extensively within the schools. This meditation technique seeks to take the individual beyond the earthly experience and into the profundity of life beyond the veil of three-dimensional physical life.

Trans-meditation, when practiced correctly, crosses the boundary between this world and the next, allowing the initiates to rise above the physical plane and make journeys to other places in their astral bodies. The astral body is also referred to as the *ba* and is the part of an individual that is not confined to a physical reality. Before beginning the trans-meditative journeys, students are coached for many years so that both their body and their soul are ready for the deep experiences of the transcendental escape. The students' physical bodies must be fit and healthy, because they can spend hours—or even days in the case of the high-initiates—in a transcendental meditative state. The body must function at an optimum level so that this time without food, water, and exercise does not impact it too heavily.

In addition, the students' levels of awareness must be advanced. They must be prepared for astral ascension and able to make the most of the experience. The initiates are introduced into trans-meditative practices at Level 4, and their first full trans-meditation in the sacred valleys marks their initiation as *pharas*—into Level 5.

While students who experience a trans-meditative release can have vastly different journeys from one another, they are coached to fulfill specific functions through their astral travels. Most of these functions are associated with gaining a better understanding of why they are alive and clarifying the purpose of their earthly existence. Certain aspects of the Mysteries are never explained to the initiates within the school system, because they are required to gain a superior understanding of themselves during the meditative journeys and return with this understanding to their physical lives.

We are going to take this opportunity to relay the experiences of one of our female students. On return from her first intergalactic trans-meditative experience, she recorded the journey; we think it nicely illustrates the real intent of this meditative technique.

> *And I am out—above my body and above the world. I am flying swiftly towards the river Negeb. I am flying as a hawk. It has kindly facilitated me as a carrier of astral souls between this world and the next. This is one of the hawk's jobs, and it loves to serve. Thank you, hawk!*
>
> *It is night, and from this vantage I can see through the hawk's eyes to the scenes below. As we move quickly towards the river Negeb, I can see the roofs of houses and some people busy in their tasks. I know that they are unaware I am above them and watching. We are over the river! It is beautiful, so beautiful! We turn swiftly to follow its course downstream, flying strongly over the water. There is a cool breeze, and the moon and stars are bright. I want to stay like this forever. I have never felt so free.*

The hawk is quickly ascending towards the skies. I encourage this motion—as I go higher, I feel freer and freer. The bird takes me as high as it can go—to the veil that separates the physical world of our planet from the heavens. And then the bird releases me to the skies—into the embrace of the Great Sky Vulture. The Vulture does not collect me like the hawk did, but I become part of his world. He exists as the great band of stars and sky above our planet, and I fly into it. At this moment, I leave the hawk behind me as he descends back into his earthly life. I have a newly acquired pair of wings! They are great vulture's wings below my arms and they propel me deeper into our galaxy. The wings are a gift from the Sky Vulture. Thank you Vulture!

I fly higher and higher on my great beautiful wings. Deeper and deeper into the heart of the galaxy—the Vulture—I go. At last I feel the energy of the Great Central Sun on my head. Its beautiful shining rays envelop me in a luminous light so gentle that I stop my flight. The light of the Great Central Sun is not like our earthly sun, which can burn the skin. The Central Sun's light is soft but still penetrating. It is like being showered with angelic flames, and I spin and spin with my arms and wings spread wide. I stay in one place spinning and spinning, and laughing and laughing with the Great Central Sun shining from above and over me. In the recesses of my mind, I know I am being naughty because I have a specific task to fulfill on this journey into the heavens, and I am delaying it. I want to fly and spin like this for ever and ever!

Eventually, my conscience gets the better of me, and I start looking around for some intended destination. Then I notice an *extremely bright star to the west-southwest of universal north. I slowly begin flying in that direction. I am not sure what I am going to find, but something inside me urges me onwards towards this unknown destination. As I get closer to the star, I begin flying faster and faster. I know now that it is the Dog-Star, Sirius. The star is getting closer, and bigger and brighter. Its light-gravity seems to be pulling me into it. I am almost there, I am almost there. What bright light! And then suddenly, on either side of the star appear the two figures of Thoth—giant figures opposing but facing one another. Between them they hold the star, which is not really a star at all. The Thoths are holding a circular Flower of Life light-grid. Sirius is not a star, it is a universal portal!*

*As I make this realization, the Flower of Life disc suddenly bulges outwards and envelops me. I am through the portal, between the two Thoths, and a brilliant bright light blinds me for a few moments, and then a scene becomes evident. It appears I am back on Earth. How boring! But on closer inspection, I realize that it is not Earth, it just appears that way. I am in a manicured garden with many paths, and on my left stands a large temple that is a sandy stone color. There are people milling around and doing their own thing. They are dressed as if in ancient Babylonian times; in long modest robes of gentle colors. They ignore me—perhaps they cannot see me? I don't think they can see me, or are not interested in me. Then I notice that a woman with a large soft auburn bun of hair and a long peach robe is aware of my presence. She does not look at me, but walks towards the temple, and I realize that I should follow—and I do.*

*I remember that her name is Mahindra and that we are in*

the complex of Akasha, where all the records of all the souls in the universe are kept. We are not on Earth. As we leave the gardens of Akasha and enter a passage of the temple, I regret that I cannot stay outside and play in the sunshine. Following her, I notice the black-and-white checked tiles of the floor of the corridor. It is like the floor of the passages in the temples of the Mysterie Schools! Black-and-white checks—reflecting the dualistic light and dark energies of the universe. Mahindra still does not look back and turns right, down a short passage and then into a tightly winding flight of stairs. The stairwell is dark and cold, and I would much rather be outside in the gardens in the sunlight. Mahindra seems very stern and just continues downwards, until we reach the basement libraries of Akasha where the soul records are kept.

She doesn't access my records but provides me with a scroll parchment and a quill pen. She takes a seat on one side of a desk and I take a seat on the other. She still hasn't spoken to me, and she looks stern and irritable. Oh dear, why? I anticipate that she expects me to record on the parchment my earthly purpose, and the reason I am alive on the planet. Oh dear, I am not one hundred percent sure. She is looking intently and sternly into my face. Why is she so solemn? I look past her and envision the great heavens that exist beyond Akasha. For a time, I am back in the Vulture, spinning and playing in the Central Sun's light. I fly on a little, looking this way and that for my purpose. I fly as a vulture—deeper and deeper into the galaxy—but nothing really occurs to me except that I feel lonely. Another vulture comes to mirror my flight and breast-to-breast we continue moving deeper into the galaxy of stars. I am still unsure.

*I move through all the recesses of my mind trying to find the answer to who I am. I pretend to be a god and swell myself to greatness. The vision dissolves—it is not true for me. I imagine myself as all sorts of things—and in all sorts of roles on the Earth. They all dissolve—they are not true for me. I just feel lonely—that's all really. I am flying again as a double vulture, breast-to-breast, contemplating who I might be. I know that my time is getting short. I can hear the singing bowl's sounds far away, and I know that it is preparing me for my return to Earth and my physical body.*

*O dear, I return to the desk with Mahindra. She is still observing me solemnly. I suggest a few ideas to her that I had on the outer plane. She stares me out—her face not flinching. I am this ... I am that ... I try some of my imaginings. She remains unmoving and unaccepting. And then I look into my heart—that place where the answers really sleep. And on my scroll I begin to write. With my quill I simply state that I am lonely, and I want to return to Earth because my true heart's love is there waiting for me. It is only a few lines long, and the rest of the parchment remains empty. That is all, I believe, simply that is all.*

*I look up and Mahindra is positively beaming at me! This must be it then—this is the simple heart-statement of my incarnation upon the Earth. She whisks my parchment away in glee, to file it where it belongs. It seems that I have got this purpose wrong in a number of incarnations, and she becomes annoyed when her clients evade their true heart's desire. She also finally speaks to me and gives me a bit more information. She explains that while I have other tasks to do on Earth, I am very aware of these and am well on-track with the various activities. I* can be commended for this. She explains that the most important reason for my incarnation is to come together with my true heart's love and that he is waiting for me on the Earth plane. She tells me how old he is. I realize that most souls have to complete many parchments of their Purpose Scrolls when they are in Akasha, and they carefully fill in many details of their soul's desire. They return to Earth with many reasons of why they are alive and what they need to do. I realize how fortunate I am that I have only a single scroll containing just a few lines!

It is time to go, and we leave the temple. Thank you Mahindra! I exit the portal and return to the Earth. On my journey back I can hear the singing bowl calling me and assisting me with finding my way home.

We, as this initiate's priests and priestesses, really love her particular example. We feel that the individual's soul personality shines through in her story and truly reflects her earthly personality. There is an aspect of the Mysteries that we always struggle to communicate to our students: However things are for us on Earth, so shall they be in death—or any other altered reality in which we find ourselves after we pass on from an earthly life. Our souls and external conditions don't change much when we pass from life. So, for example, if we are childlike and love freedom in life—as is the case with this particular soul—so shall it be after life. If we are serious and methodical upon the Earth, so shall we be between lives.

The only thing that separates a soul from its soul home is the physical body. As can be seen from the above example of astral traveling, the body can easily be transcended for temporary periods.

We do not, however, condone the practice of transcendental meditation without limits. We have found that individuals who spend too long out of their bodies become addicted to the feeling and ungrounded in their earthly life. This is not the purpose of trans-meditation; in fact, it is contradictory to what the schools aim to achieve. Mystical meditation aims to sharpen the initiates' awareness of universal life, life on Earth, and their unique roles within life. So in essence, trans-meditation serves to deepen the connection between students and their earthly lives.

Another reason we like this particular example is that the young female student manages to strip away the falsities of her ego. There is an unfortunate consequence of the school system, in that so much focus on spiritual development often creates a kind of spiritual egoism amongst the students. Part of our teachings is that we are all pieces of the god-energy, and all exist to somehow facilitate the evolution of the divine. Living in awareness of this fact, it is easy for individual students to start believing they are superior to others who have not accepted their divine existence. This falsely exalted attitude is detrimental to true soul evolution and spiritual mastery. So, students often need to be knocked off their pedestals before they can attain lasting illumination.

There are several ways in which the students might be humiliated. (Please note that our use of the term *humiliate* does not hold the negative modern-day connotations that you might be used to. To be humiliated within our school system is considered quite a positive process, a healthy step to pass through on ascension up the pyramid of enlightenment.)

First, the student might fail an initiation test that would have moved them up to a higher level of learning. As mentioned, these tests are objective, and so their own soul is saying, "You are not ready to go further in the universal Mysteries at this time." Examination failures often have a very humiliating effect on individuals. If they are wise, they will accept their failure and return at another time to try again.

A second form of humiliation might be an event that happens within the initiate's ordinary life. For example, they may have a handicap or an accident; they may have their heart broken; they may lose all of their possessions and money; or one of their loved ones may pass on. These might all seem like unpleasant events, but to true seekers of the Mysteries it is a great honor to experience such encumbrances. Being humiliated is a sure sign that the soul is ready to strip away the falsities of the material world and embrace the divinity of a spiritually holistic life. This does not mean that the individual must remain in suffering or poverty—not at all—but once they have drawn the lesson from the humiliating experience, their souls are free to reap the best of what life has to offer thereafter through full spiritual consciousness.

Coming back to our example: the young student was not overtly egotistical, but she also was not completely in touch with her reason for being alive. During the trans-meditation flight, she went through a number of iterations of who she might be and what her role in life could be. None of these considerations made her feel happy; none of them were true for her. Eventually, she looked deeply into her heart and into the most mundane part of herself—the simplest, most uncomplicated piece of herself. From here, she received her answers.

The answer of our soul's purpose is often so obvious that we don't accept it at first. The best way to uncover it is to sit in a quiet corner or under the shade of a tree in the garden. Then, if we write down in absolute secrecy the thing, or things, that we truly want to be or experience, we may have our answers. It is best to destroy this piece of paper afterwards because our soul's purpose is the absolute secret of our life. It is a condition of the human mind to question and judge; by revealing who we are to others, we can skew our own pure perceptions of what we know to be correct.

Our young student had been very diligent in life, and so she didn't have much to uncover with her mentor in the Akashic spiritual complex. Still, it was the thing she finally wrote down, which was the final piece of the puzzle that her soul required for illumination on the physical plane. And this is a secret: *it is always that thing, or those things, that will make us most happy that are the keys to our spiritual evolution.* The mystery is to know what will make us so happy. We often confuse ourselves and allow the ego to take control, thereby denying the entreaties of the soul. Some souls do aspire to material greatness, power, dominion over others, and extreme wealth; others do not. The objective of transcendental meditation is for the soul to truly know, believe, and then act-out their life's purpose.

▼

If the student is successful in her trans-meditative journey (which is often to Akasha), she is considered to have attained the Purpose Scrolls. Many of our statues and glyphs are of initiates holding the scrolls in their hands, symbolic of the attainment of their purpose. (See image at the beginning of chapter 11.) When our young initiate returned to her physical body, she was commended with one of the highest initiation levels of the Mysterie Schools. If she wished, she could have continued with the

# Trans-Meditation

priestess training. However, her final success would have lain in her ability to seek out and connect with the man who was waiting patiently for her on the Earth plane. Herein lies the true meaning of the Mysteries—*there is no mystery so great as the truth we hide from ourselves.*

The vehicle that facilitates the initiates on their trans-meditation journeys is the meditation casket, box, or sarcophagus. These are generally large rectangular or oval containers made of granite, basalt, or quartzite. The sarcophagi are extremely heavy and solid with plenty of room inside for the student to lie down and stretch out. A flat lid of the same material sits on top of the base in which the student lies. The lid is also extremely heavy.

The caskets are inscribed with glyphs describing the meditative journey as well as the initiates' own life journeys. On the inside of the cover of the boxes may be inscribed a representation of the sky goddess, whom you will know as Nut. This is a metaphor for how the student becomes part of the heavenly sky, which is mostly a female construct. At the head of the casket basin may be an image of the student's astral body supporting the wings of the vulture. This image is often repeated at the foot of the casket and called Isis, which means life. (See chapter 12, Isis.) The vulture flight is also a mostly feminine concept because of the connection to Isis. (See chapter 12, Nekhabet, the Sky Vulture.)

The solidity of the meditation caskets protects the students' physical bodies from harm while they trans-meditate. It is nearly impossible to move the sarcophagi, or lift the lids, with human strength alone. We have very interesting methods of transporting these caskets—and raising and lowering the lids. We use the same principle that was used by our predecessors to build the pyramids and many of our temples. That principle is sound harmonization, also known as vibrational chiseling when used for building. Quite simply, sound forms a vibrational wave through the air. The correct sounds can create such an intense wave that the resultant force may be used for all sorts of purposes, such as masonry or moving objects.

We use the resonating ball tablets, which are a gift from the Hathors, to move the meditation sarcophagi as well as to raise and lower the lids. The resonating ball tablets are solid rectangular tables, whose surfaces contain hollows arranged symmetrically like a game board. Inside these hollows fit round balls, about the size of four fists. The tablet and the balls are made of a dense material, similar to granite, which is not found on your planet. The activation of the balls allows them to move vertically up and down in resonation, above the template surface. The resonating balls are activated by electro-magnetism, using tools brought to Iyrgr by the Atlantian ancestors. In this state of vibration, the balls are independently suspended above the physical surface and allowed to undulate at a certain frequency. The balls can be played like a musical instrument. The music of these spheres creates specific sound waves through the air, which can raise the caskets for transportation and allow them to hover and move horizontally onto a waiting barge or onto a meditation platform. The sound balls can also raise and lower the heavy lids so that the students can enter and exit their sarcophagi.

The students design and carve their own sarcophagi once they reach a particular level of the Mysterie teachings. Typically, this work is done within the temple compounds, and the initiates may be busy for years perfecting their caskets. They generally are

# Trans-Meditation

expected to use their own sarcophagi for trans-meditation, but in some instances they may use one of the practice caskets or permanent caskets. Examples of permanent meditation caskets are those that remain fixed within the three great pyramids on the plateau next to the Negeb. These cannot be removed from the confines of the pyramidal structures; once the initiates reach the highest level of learning (Level 7) before becoming pharaohs, they are required to trans-meditate from one of the three great pyramids.

Although it is true that trans-meditation can be practiced anywhere, and at any time, the Mystical Schools have established a well-rehearsed system for the students to achieve maximum results from their meditations. When first learning how to trans-meditate, the students usually activate this state from within their bedchambers at night or from another secure location within the temples. They do not use sarcophagi at this point. As they progress, the chambers within the sacred valleys are used. These chambers are spacious alcoves dug deep into the rock below pyramidal-shaped mountains. We use two valleys on the west bank of the Negeb, opposite Karnak, which each contain about a dozen meditation tombs. These valleys are used for the trans-meditation initiation into Level 5—the attainment of the status *phara*. At this level the students use their own sarcophagi, which are transported along the Negeb on the sacred barges, or barques.

From the barques, the sarcophagi are moved by sound through the Colossi of Memnon and into one of the sacred valleys. The Colossi are a pair of immense sitting statues that guard the entrance to our sacred valleys and are aligned to the summer solstice sunrise. The caskets are then interred on a meditation platform inside one of the alcoves of the valleys. The initiate, amongst a procession of students and priests/priestesses, will accompany her sarcophagus into the alcove.

The alcoves are accessed via long, open corridors that have been decorated with glyphs for the occasion of trans-mediation. These include the records of the individual students. Many vertical rows of repeating glyphs show how particular initiates have passed through the various requirements and lessons needed to bring them to the point of mastery. When an initiate is ready for a trans-meditative experience in the valleys, the meditation and meditation ritual are considered the initiation processes to be proclaimed a phara—or master. If the initiation is successful, he may continue with his studies towards becoming a pharaoh (one who can in turn teach the Mysteries). When he is ready to be initiated as a pharaoh, his trans-meditative initiation takes place within one of the three great pyramids.

The pyramidal structure is ideal for trans-meditation for a number of reasons. First, it focuses the energies of the individuals enabling them to leave their bodies successfully. Second, it protects the individuals from psychic harm during trans-meditation. Third, the pyramid maintains an optimal state of health for the physical body and creates a protective structure around the entombed. Fourth, the pyramidal energies facilitate a deep and trans-personal journey for the students; and fifth, the pyramid assists in guiding the astral body home.

Trans-meditation requires the astral body to freely exit and return to the physical body; it also requires that the physical body remains safe and healthy while the astral body is journeying. Psychic protection of the initiate's astral body is also essential. Deep meditation can lead to bad experiences if the correct procedures are not followed. A pyramid creates an electro-magnetic gravitational field, like a vortex, which acts mostly on an invisible energetic level. The objects, or persons, within the pyramid are contained in this energy vortex, reducing the impact of external environmental factors and foreign, harmful energies. A pyramid is also an impenetrable physical structure with few access points. The sheer immensity of the great pyramids of Iyrgr, as well as the pyramidal mountains in the valleys, increases the strength of their energy vortexes. When aligned with heavenly light-bodies (as explained in chapter 6), the pyramids absorb the full intensity of the sedjes, and their energetic strength is further concentrated. Transcendental meditation requires the initiate to reach a semi-comatose state in which the physical functioning of the body drops to abnormally low levels; metabolism virtually ceases. In this state, the initiates are vulnerable to physical harm, deteriorating health, psychic attack, and even death. The pyramids assist in maintaining protection on a number of levels, as well as ensuring optimal health during trans-meditation, which can last for many hours or several days.

Naturally, being entombed in a stone box with an immovable lid within an immense pyramidal structure can be a terrifying experience for the unprepared. Initiates must be well and truly ready for the metaphysical experience of astral traveling; tests are conducted before students are permitted to enter into deep trans-meditative states. As ascended priests and priestesses of the Mysteries, we remember our first experiences of trans-meditation well. It is as exhilarating as it is frightening; if experienced properly, it is heavenly sustenance for the soul experiencing a physical incarnation.

For the initiations—whether in the valleys or the pyramids—a solemn procedure is arranged to transport the initiates and their caskets to their destinations.

For the valley initiations, alcoves have been dug deep into the pyramidal mountains and are accessed via decorated corridors. Allowance is made for only one initiate per alcove, although a number of initiates may be using the valley at once—each in their appointed alcove. Each student's sarcophagus is positioned in the middle of the meditation alcove on the meditation platform. Surrounding the platform are four low pillars that support electro-magnetic activators that facilitate the sound harmonization process for the raising and lowering of the granite lids of the sarcophagi. These activators act to set up a three-dimensional pyramidal electro-magnetic vortex around the casket for energetic protection during trans-meditation. This energy pyramid protects the initiate from physical and psychic harm during meditation.

Before entering the meditation casket, the initiates are prepared for their journeys. They are anointed with essences and oils from canopic jars that stand on an anointing table. Holy incenses are burned, and many incantations are recited to request protection for both the astral body, that it may depart and return safely to the physical body, and the physical body, that it may emerge safely into the light of day.

The valley initiations usually last only through one night. The ceremony begins after nightfall and includes selected pharaohs (priests/priestesses) and initiates who assist with every aspect of the process of facilitating the initiate into trans-meditation. Besides the powerful scents of the natural essences and incenses used within the ceremony, beautiful sounds and harmonics are played on singing bowls, drums, and other sound instruments. All this is in order for the initiate to relax and more easily connect to the heavens and experience the astral journey. Certain harmonics (which act to induce a hypnotic-like state) enable the physical body to be calm and the astral body to depart. Once the initiate has reached a fairly deep level of meditation, the granite lid is closed, using the resonating balls. Everybody leaves the chamber and exits the corridor. The entrance is shut with great stone blocks—once again moved through sound harmonization. A single sentry, who is the guiding pharaoh of the initiate, will remain through the night to guard the entrance.

The next day, the small ceremonial party will return and enter the meditation alcove. The singing bowl will once again be used to draw the astral body back into the physical body. The lid will be raised by sound and the vital signs of the initiate checked—he should be conscious with his eyes open at this stage. After this, many of the party, except for the guiding pharaoh, will withdraw. The initiate is allowed plenty of time to surface from his experience. There is often a separate little alcove in which he will receive water and fruit to help stabilize his physical body. After some incantations for reemergence into the daylight, the initiate is free to leave the alcove, accompanied by his pharaoh.

The great pyramid initiations are similar but much deeper. The vibrational frequency of the mammoth structures allows the astral body of the initiate to be projected deep into the heavens and stay there for a few days of Earth time—while the physical body remains protected within the pyramid. The formal ceremony takes an initiate along the Negeb on a holy barge from one of the various temples. Again, only a few select attendees will accompany the student into the pyramid. They will enter through the main, north-facing, entrance and follow the inclines into the grand central chamber in which all the initiation ceremonies will be performed. The main entrance to the pyramid is blocked from the inside immediately upon entering the corridor so that the preparation ceremony may be conducted in sanctity and safety.

Once the initiation ceremony has been performed and the initiate is entombed, the small group will exit the pyramid through the descending viaduct, which is a secret passage leading to a concealed exit. It is vital that the individual within the pyramid remains safe, because her physical body is prone to harm when she exists in a trans-meditative state. This is particularly true during the pyramid journeys, because of the intensity of the stone structures and the depth of the experience of the meditator within them. The initiates reach such a profound level of meditation that your modern-day doctors would likely pronounce them to be no longer living. However, according to the Mysteries, a person who does not breathe and whose heart does not beat is not considered dead—it is when the divine luminous cord that connects the astral body to the physical body is broken that a person is considered to have moved on from the physical world. Therefore, during trans-meditation, we consider the initiates to be completely alive and vital. It is just that transcendental meditation facilitates a death-like experience as well as all the incumbent opportunities for enlightenment and resurrection. In fact, coming forth by day—when the initiate leaves her tomb—feels like being born again, with new and profound insight into why she is alive.

The *ba* is the astral body in motion. It is not quite the same thing as the soul or the spiritual body. The soul is timeless and cannot die. The spiritual body consists of both the ba and the soul—it exists simultaneously on Earth and in the spiritual realms. The ba, or astral body, connects the soul to the physical body. When a person is considered to be no longer living, his ba has left his physical body, taking the soul with it. The ba is required for incarnation into life, while the soul is the entity that is present both within life and between lives. The ba is the ethereal imprint of the physical body and is only able to travel when the ka—or personal energy vibration—of the individual is high enough.

Although we do not like to talk about it, it is possible for the astral body never to return to the physical body during trans-meditation, especially if the physical body experiences some shock while the astral body is absent. However, in the many thousands of years of the Mysterie Schools, death of an initiate has been almost unheard of. Every initiate who partakes of trans-meditation is carefully trained over years for the experience, her physical and spiritual body prepared exquisitely closer to the time of meditation, and her physical body protected and watched over during her journey. Also, the priests and priestesses are able to request or facilitate spiritual protection for the initiate during meditation—which is usually provided from the ethereal dimensions of space. All this work is conducted by the pharaohs who have experienced the various initiations themselves. As with the valley initiations, the guiding pharaoh of the pyramid initiate will be present when the individual awakens and will lead her into the recovery room below the central meditation alcove within the pyramidal structure. The initiate may stay in the recovery room with her priestess for as long as she needs, and then they will both exit through the secret passage to the outside world.

◆

You may wonder why the three great pyramids are different sizes. First, the pyramids are symbolic of the holy family or trinity—father, mother, child. Second, the pyramids are aligned with the heavens, as explained in chapter 6. This provides the cosmic with some idea of the intent of the initiate whose astral body is being transported. The three great pyramids are aligned with the three stars forming Orion's belt, and so mimic their sizes. They also contain shafts that run from the outside faces high up the pyramidal surfaces and into the central meditation chambers. These shafts are oriented to various other fixed star-portals. In essence, this alignment assists the astral bodies of the initiates to journey to the relevant cosmic location for their own particular trans-meditative experience. Since the location of the pyramids reflects various heavenly bodies, the journey of the ba from within the pyramid to the cosmic can be likened to *bringing the heavens down to Earth*.

Within the Mysterie Schools we teach that time and space do not exist, and so we see no difference between the ascension of an astral body and the descent of the heavens to Earth. In other words, where and how these two realities meet is of little consequence. We can believe that the astral body makes a journey into the skies, but we can also believe that the astral body remains where it is and the heavens descend to the Earth plane. The ba joins the heavens in an altered reality whether it exists within the physical space of the planet or not.

As explained in the example of the young female initiate, the star Sirius is an intergalactic portal (which is expanded upon in chapter 6). This can be likened to a universal airport that allows objects to project themselves instantaneously to various places in the universe. The example given was of an astral body that was transported from our galaxy (the Vulture Galaxy) to the Akashic complex, which exists in an entirely different part of the universe. The thing that allows this instantaneous transfer from one place to another is intent. If the astral body is on a journey into the skies with the intent of uncovering its soul's purpose, it will naturally gravitate towards Akasha—if it is appropriate. It is one of the universal laws that *what we desire, we acquire.*

Therefore, the three great pyramids are arranged so that the full intent of the entombed initiate is known beforehand. At least, the intended destination of the initiate is known. For example, the great pyramid will take the astral body most easily to Alnitak, one of the three stars of Orion's belt, or to the Pole Star, Thuban. Mother pyramid leads most easily to the Alnilam star of Orion and baby pyramid to the Mintaka star of Orion.

In chapter 6 we explained that many of the fixed stars visible from the Earth are not celestial bodies at all but are intense light-emitting universal portals. This refers to the stars aligned with the great pyramids and many of the temples. When the students trans-meditate, their astral bodies are pulled naturally towards the portal that aligns best with their soul's intent. The initiates reflect upon their intent prior to entering the trans-meditative state. In fact, the initiates are compelled to discuss the exact nature of their intent with their guiding priests/priestesses to clarify why they are embarking on trans-meditation.

Trans-meditation can be undertaken randomly, but we have

found this to be a dangerous practice if the astral body is not guided by the higher objective of the individual's soul. Our student in the example needed a reminder of the main reason she had chosen to incarnate to Earth, and Akasha was the best place for her to go to get this information—accessed via the portal Sirius. Her trans-meditation location and time would have been selected carefully by her guiding pharaoh, according to the position and movements of Sirius in this instance.

Alternatively, one of the Orion portals, or even the Pole Star, might have been preferable. A student usually gravitates towards Thuban (the Pole Star) if there is a message for them from a very high order of beings, such as the Angels. Thuban leads the way to the most advanced life-forms in our universe; they exist mostly in the ethereal realms. The Orion's belt trinity leads to different parts of the outer universe, far away from the Vulture Galaxy. Aldebaran, in the Taurus constellation, is like a never-ending gateway to many, many worlds—including the Aldebaran planetary archipelago itself. The Aldebaran portal is like a long corridor, where doors lead off on either side to various parts of the galaxy and universe. Aldebaran is considered the adventure portal—like your Heathrow airport in London—of multitudinous options and continual busyness.

The Pleiades and Hyades are stellar archipelagos of life. They are not usually used as direct portals but are more often accessed via the Sirius or Aldebaran portals. The beings inhabiting the Pleiades and Hyades clusters have been great friends of the Earth since the experiment began. These constellations contain the planets and life-forms that are most comparable to life on Earth.

Wherever the initiates choose to go on their trans-meditative journeys, the experience remains strictly theirs. They are under no obligation to share their journeys upon return. In fact, they are encouraged to keep their findings to themselves. We, as priests and priestesses of the school system, find trans-meditation particularly exciting; no matter how much we teach our students over the decades, centuries, and millennia, we cannot pass on certain of our knowledge and wisdom except through the key of trans-meditation. Via trans-meditation, any individual can access hidden and sacred parts of the universe; more important, they can access hidden and sacred parts of themselves—and their life journeys.

# 10

## Judgement and Universal Laws

Our Mysterie Schools were most active between 10,500 and 3,000 BCE before your recorded history began. The major decline of the schools happened between 3,000 and 600 BCE, after which time the schools no longer existed as mainstream institutions within society. The teachings went underground and spread silently around the world, at first to the Mediterranean, the United Kingdom, Europe, and the Middle East. The Egyptian Mysterie compatriots joined hands secretly with disciples of other mystic institutions and movements, which still exist today. From our perspective, we are noting a rebirth of the Mysteries around the world, and a reestablishment of our old order—but this will remain largely behind the scenes. As we mentioned, our teachings are not for everybody, and only the most advanced souls will gravitate towards our prescribed path of enlightenment.

From an historical perspective, when the schools started to go into decline within Egypt, societal falsities began to permeate what we taught as truth. Because the teachings of the Mysteries were a private and orderly affair within the school system, our initiates and priests/priestesses were not permitted or able to rectify any misconceptions that began to grow within external society. The schools began to lose their power as suspicion, fear, and jealousy arose in the hearts of those not included within the schools or not at a sufficiently high level within the school system. This process happened slowly over more than 2,000 years, but it ended the golden age of our land, Iyrgr.

Our teachings—including our beliefs and rituals, healing practices, hieroglyphs, stonemasonry, and trans-meditation—became increasingly misunderstood by those not trained in the Mysteries. Later generations of Egyptians misinterpreted the trans-meditation process as worship of the afterlife and a death ritual. Quite the opposite, trans-meditation was designed to celebrate and illuminate human life. While transition through death and the spiritual world is a deeply important part of the soul journey—as taught in our schools—the main objective of the Mysteries is to illuminate the human journey through *life*. The obsession with death in Egypt during the last few thousand years of its dominance was abhorrent to us. In particular, what is now known as *The Book of the Am-Duat* or *The Book of the Dead* was and is misunderstood. It originally was a set of incantations, or affirmations, learnt by the students to protect their physical bodies during trans-meditation, to guide their astral bodies through the other worlds, and to ensure safe return to the physical world.

The incantations were learnt by heart and were not allowed to be written because of the sensitive nature of the material and the potential for confusion. It seems that later these affirmations became common knowledge and appeared in scrolls and on stonework. Out of context, the incantations of the meditative journey mean very little.

Of course, in every mistruth there is some element of truth; while the Mysterie Schools did not focus intensely on the process now known as judgement, we did teach some of the elements of the kharmic cycle, including physical death and what happens afterwards. The reason for including the kharmic cycle is that the students were enrolled within the schools in order to advance their souls towards illumination. Passing between lives, souls are subjected to a type of judgement or kharmic assessment that guides them towards illumination. This judgement is conducted in the spiritual realm with absolute love and fairness. Conclusions are based upon the soul's ultimate objective—to achieve universal kharmic balance. There is no condemnation by a series of supreme beings or devouring monsters. It is true, however, that the individual's commitment to universal truth is measured through her energetic heart-center upon transition from life, but this is the most objective and fair mechanism through which to measure results. It is also true that each soul's journey from every lifetime, and even between lives, is recorded and housed in the Akashic Temple, which is protected and overseen by Thoth. Thoth is also known as universal written and spoken truth (see chapter 12 on Egyptian gods).

▼

One of our procedures, known as the confessional, is an interesting one that is repeated a few times during the students' schooling years in order to prepare them for the kharmic balancing process post-life. Your modern-day confessionals amuse us; individuals are encouraged to confess their errors—or what they believe to be errors—to your priests. We believe this is counterproductive to a true confession. A confession within our school system is a process through which students (or even priests or priestesses) reveal to themselves how close they are to their living truth. In other words: are they living according to the will of their soul, or have they been distracted or misguided by the dictates of their ego? No priest or priestess can answer this for any other individual—students are answerable only to themselves.

The confessional uses a number of procedures in which the students may get in touch with their true natures and their higher-selves. These practices can include deep meditation; trans-meditation is considered a method of confession to the self. Within our school system, a confessional is more like a revelation than a condemnation. No punishment is issued—there is merely an expectation that students who are aware of their deviations from their true paths will remedy these.

⏽

Of course, the kharmic balancing in the spiritual realms, as well as the confessionals, naturally take into account adherence to the Universal Laws of Love. These are the objective universal codes that govern L.I.F.E., and what it represents: Love in Freedom of Expression. Evolution is the process of development as love is allowed to manifest independently through life.

As life unfolds, there is a set of causal laws that are omnipotent within universal evolution. These laws ensure a continual energetic equilibrium between all things. As evolution creates waves of change that ripple through our universe in perpetual motion, so the universal laws direct how this change needs to find homogenization, ensuring cosmic balance. The Universal Laws of Love are all-pervasive and apply—without favor—to each and every object, aspect, and individual within our universe.

For some, the laws are difficult to understand and therefore overwhelming to practice. Our advice is always this: if a person is living through their heart-center, then they are naturally obeying all of the universal laws. Therefore, even a baby can understand and apply the Universal Laws of Love. The laws also apply to inanimate objects as well as events, energies, and all aspects of universal life.

For humanity, the laws are simple. All the Universal Laws of Love fall under a single banner:

*Life is a creation to allow love expression. No part of life may exist in such a way as to destroy any other part of life.*

Therefore, under this banner could appear secondary causes of the infringement upon life: murder, theft, revenge, pollution, hatred, injury, hampering, emotional abuse, greed, and laziness.

The list of causal items is endless. In fact, such a list would continue to evolve as life continues to evolve. In this way, the factors that cause universal laws to be violated are as numerous and as ever-changing as the elements that constitute life. However, if life is lived in a way that supports the overall universal statement, the Universal Laws of Love are naturally adhered to.

Of course, there are various interpretations to the overall statement; it takes wisdom to understand how and when the destruction of life becomes real. For instance, an individual who hunts an animal for food is not violating the universal statement, but an individual who hunts an animal for sport is doing so. It is not possible for us to fully describe in this book all the ways the universal statement can be interpreted—there are scores of entities in the spiritual realms dedicated to the interpretation of life laws. As mentioned before: if choices are filtered through the heart-center, they will naturally concord with the universal statement.

Kharma is an objective and natural result of violation of (or positively, adherence to) the Universal Laws of Love. There is no controlling group or deity that exacts punishment on those who transgress the universal laws. Kharma is simply a universal movement of energies, which seeks to rectify itself and maintain harmony. Kharma acts under its own volition, in accordance with cosmic consciousness. Kharmic balancing is like the ocean tide that shifts and changes, ebbs and flows, and continually circulates according to an invisible gravitational pull. The force that guides the kharmic currents originates from a deep cosmic source, but it acts within every minute part of life. Like the moon acting from a distance and guiding the oscillating water levels around the Earth, kharma is so much more than the high and low tides we see along the shore.

Acting against the Universal Laws of Love can be readily apparent; for example, breaking a basic law of a civil society. The result can be a jail sentence. A less obvious—but no less significant—contravention might occur when an individual does not act in harmony with the highest good of all. For instance, when people marry the wrong persons because they are impatient, or marry them for the wrong reasons, they act against the natural flow of things. This affects not only themselves but multitudes because marriage, like all actions, affects the whole of creation. The results of an incorrect marriage may include an unhappy marriage in that lifetime, relationship difficulties in another lifetime, or any number of misfortunes.

Kharma will restore the balance when the conditions are right for particular individuals, when they are most ready to learn the far-reaching consequences of their actions. The kharmic results may be positive or negative, depending on the particular cause of a kharmic reaction.

We will not be providing a current list of the universal law statements that derive from the overarching statement above. This is because, out of context, these laws can be confusing and open to misunderstanding. Universal laws are sacred; they need to be communicated and interpreted within the correct spiritual framework. However, as mentioned, if human beings are operating from their heart-center, then they are in a continual state of living according to the Universal Laws of Love.

# 11

## Representations of Initiations Passed

Since much of the work of the Mysterie Schools is invisible, we use symbols to represent the initiations that have been passed. These are generally items of clothing or adornment such as painted eyes of kohl, pleated skirts and head-dresses, diadems for the head, staffs, and crowns. These symbols may be physical pieces of clothing or jewelry, or they may be symbolic images that only appear on statues and hieroglyphs.

Above is a statue from Karnak Temple. This initiate wears the *nemset* head-dress as well as the cobra diadem. The initiate's eyes are painted with kohl, and he is wearing the chin-strap piece. Around the student's waist is the pleated skirt with the Peace ovoculum on the buckle of the belt. The initiate holds his Purpose Scrolls in both hands and his left leg is forward.

Some of the initiatory items represent which levels of learning have been passed, and some symbols show certain attainments that do not belong to a specific level. The actual items can sometimes be worn everyday (like the pleated skirts or kohl) or only at ceremonies (such as the chin-strap attachment or one of the crowns).

One of the themes evident in our symbolic life is the overcoming of duality—in other words, finding harmony within the human form. Wherever alternating stripes of black (or blue) and gold (or white) appear, these are symbolic of finding balance in duality. The human is an incarnate being who has equal potential to express his or her light and dark sides. Humankind exists simultaneously as both a physical and spiritual creation. We do not believe that one or the other side of these polar opposites is any better than the other—it is finding an equilibrium between the continually alternating pillars of human existence that is important. Overall, the spiritual or upper life may be represented by the color gold, the lotus, the white upper crown, or the vulture. The lower or physical life is indicated by the color blue (or black), the papyrus, the red lower crown, or the snake.

## Eyes of Kohl

All students who are accepted into the schools may wear dark kohl around their eyes and on their eyebrows. The kohl mimics the eye coloration of the Hathors, who originally taught the Mysteries in ancient Egypt. The kohl also reflects the Eye of Horus or the All-Seeing Eye (see chapter 16).

Wearing the kohl means that the initiate has a true intent to seek out the answers to life's questions and the mystery of themselves—they are a *sedjater*. If students leave the school system, they must cease to wear the kohl.

The eyes of kohl image appears in chapter 1.

## Armband Amulets on Wrists and on Upper Arms

The armbands show how the student's actions are guided by a higher purpose, which originates from the heart. The armbands can be awarded within the first years of learning, usually within Level 3.

## Shoulder Collar

The multi-layered collar that rests on the shoulders is usually white and gold, but it may contain the primary colors. The collar shows how the sun shining from above anoints the initiate with its rays. The shoulder collar reminds the students how the light of the Great Central Sun—cosmic light—shines down upon them as they go about their spiritual business. The students may wear an actual collar attachment if they desire at any stage in their training. See shoulder collar in the image under the Pleated Skirt item below.

See the introduction of chapter 12 for an explanation of the Great Central Sun.

## The Staff (Crook) and Flail

The staff, also called the crook, and flail loosely mean to serve and to protect. The staff is an image of divine service in humility (chapter 14), and the flail is a defense weapon to protect the sacred path. Neither the crook nor the flail are used within daily life in the schools; they are symbolic only. A staff and flail may be awarded to certain students to remind them of the symbolism of these objects.

Since Osiris means *service to life*, the staff and flail can also be called the Osirian scepters. See chapter 12 for Osiris.

## The Purpose Scrolls

Attainment of the Purpose Scrolls is explained in chapter 9.

Post trans-meditation, high-initiates return to their earthly bodies imbued with cosmic intelligence and a deeper knowledge of themselves and their life purpose. From the halls of Akasha, the initiates are likely to have gained their Purpose Scrolls—scrolls inscribed in their own hand containing the purpose of their earthly existence.

While it is impossible to bring back physical items from trans-meditation, the scrolls are included symbolically in almost all of our statues; both hands are closed around stone scrolls or around gaps in which representative papyrus scrolls may be inserted. The scrolls of the statues remind the students in their daily lives about the importance of their individual earthly purposes.

## Matted Wig

The matted wig worn behind the ears does not have a particular mystical symbolism. It is a continuation from the tradition of the Hathors, who do not have hair; when they came to the Earth to teach the Mysteries, they wore wigs to appear as human as possible.

Hathor with wig and the Djed-platform.

## Skullcap

The skullcap is usually blue or black; it is a symbol of service and truth. The skullcap also represents the attainment of *ptah* (see chapter 2). *Ptah* is further explained in chapter 12.

## Chin-strap Attachment

The chin-strap attachment, or false beard, is symbolic of the fact that the initiate only seeks and speaks the truth. When the initiates understand truth or *maat* (see ovoculum, chapter 15), they are permitted to wear the false beard—even just for a day—to remind them to filter all their speech through the avenue of truth.

## Pleated Head-dress

The pleated head-dress, also called the *nemset* or *nemes* head-dress, is often alternating gold and blue/black showing the overcoming of duality. The nemset resembles the ladder of light (chapter 8), and is symbolic of the stage of illumination when the student becomes a *phara* (Level 4). The nemset is also called the pharonic crown and may be worn in real life as a folded, pleated cloth. The pharonic crown works together with the pleated skirt, as described below.

## Pleated Skirt

The pharonic head-dress and skirt (or dress) together emulate a pyramid—specifically a pyramid of light. The pleated skirt, also called the pyramidal skirt of the hieroglyphs, may be worn by the pharaohs who have completed the pyramid initiation. In the case of women, they will wear a pleated dress. The pleats represent the alternating currents of light and dark, and the shape of the skirts/dresses is that of a pyramid. When worn with the pharonic crown, the initiates appear to be wearing the pyramid. In other words, they have attained illumination, the top of the pyramid; they have become the pyramid.

Only pharaohs who have completed Level 7 may wear both the *nemset* and the pleated robes together.

Some exaggerated versions of the pleated pyramidal skirt appear on hieroglyphs. The skirt is pointed forward to such a degree that it looks as if the initiate is rising from the pyramid itself. The rays of the sun are shining from the angle of the pyramid. The individual is also wearing a shoulder collar, as explained above. This image completes the metaphor.

## Cobra and Vulture Diadem

The diadem is worn around the crown of the head so that the vulture and snake images are above the third-eye in the middle of the forehead (over the sixth, or psychic, chakra). The diadem often accompanies the nemset sheath.

The vulture—a symbol of the *upper* spiritual life—reminds the initiates that they are part of the Great Sky Vulture (see chapter 12) and the evolution of eternal spiritual life that the vulture embodies. By wearing the vulture on the diadem, students take it upon themselves to uphold the way of the vulture.

The cobra—a representation of the *lower* earthly, or physical, world—is symbolic of the initiate's ability to see life through the eyes of a snake. The *phara* observes life with the perfect clarity and wisdom of the snake god, Memnon. (See chapter 12, Memnon.)

The schools have a number of diadems available for ceremonies. These circlets are exquisitely made from precious metals and materials, such as gold and lapis lazuli; they are encrusted with jewels. We like the students to experience a physical diadem at least once in their schooling, since it materializes the symbolism as described above. The initiate may attain the diadem symbol at any time up until the completion of Level 4 after which stage, it is a compulsory requirement for becoming a *phara*.

## Vulture/Falcon Head-dress

The vulture or the falcon head-dress is an image reserved for statues and glyphs. It has acquired the same meaning as the Sky Vulture or the Falcon. See chapter 12, Nekhabet and Horus.

## Crowns

### The Djed-platform

The Djed and the Djed-platform are explained and illustrated in chapter 3. The Djed-platform acts as a base for the various crowns that are part of the school symbolism. (The platform is illustrated under the Matted Wig item of this section.)

The Djed-platform shows that individuals have achieved balance between their emotional, physical, mental, and spiritual selves; it must be attained by Level 4 before *phara*-ship. The platform also announces that the initiate has achieved a stable internal world upon which various other achievements may be built. Many of the symbolic crowns of the Mysteries are placed upon the Djed-platform.

The crowns are usually symbolic and only appear in glyphs and on statues. However, crowns may be worn to ceremonies on occasion. Although the Djed-platform must be attained by the completion of Level 4, the remaining crowns may be achieved at any time throughout an initiate's schooling. We conduct small ceremonies when the students understand, and embody, the symbolism of the various crowns described below.

### The Upper Crown

The crown of the upper or spiritual world is white and reflects the color of the crown chakra (explained in chapter 7). The crown has a light-source shape because it shows how the wearers draw on heavenly inspiration and concentrate the luminescence of the cosmic in their physical embodiment every day.

### The Lower Crown

The crown of the lower or material world is red and reflects the color of the base chakra. The crown has a squarish base, intended to show the earthly solidity of its nature, and extends up the back in symbolism of how the wearer aspires to reach cosmic illumination through a physical body. The proboscis loop on the lower crown is a reflection of the proboscis on the Eye of Horus (see chapter 16) and is a symbol of everlasting spiritual sensitivity.

### The Combined Crown

The combination of the upper and lower crowns symbolizes that the wearers have achieved mastery in both their physical and spiritual lives. They therefore live in a continual state of balance as spiritual beings, incarnated in physical bodies, completing spiritual work. The initiate is connected to, and has mastered, Heaven and Earth.

### The Double Crown

The Double Crown is a tall two-pronged crown decorated with colored layers. This is the crown of duality, and celebrates the human being in physical form. The layers of color up the crown are usually the three primaries, as discussed in chapter 7. Sometimes the sundisc is embedded at the base of the crown, showing how duality has been overcome.

The Double Crown shows balance of all polar energies—left and right, yin and yang, male and female, light and dark—and reaches up to connect with the heavens through this balance from the Djed-platform.

### The Uraeus Crown

The Uraeus is a cobra crowned with the sundisc, as explained in chapter 16. The Uraeus Crown is a ring of cobras crowned with suns. This crown indicates that the initiate is a permanently open channel for divine wisdom and cosmic intelligence. See chapter 12, Memnon.

### The Crowning Crown

The Crowning Crown may take many forms, but it is often a combination of items. The articles may include other types of crown shown above, as well as those items described below:

The goat's horns are a platform of divine masculinity and strength. They represent the servant of the Sun God, Khnum, and the quiet but determined strength he shows in exercising his spirituality in the manifested world. The goat itself is a gentle but strong creature. The horns are illustrated in chapter 16, and Khnum is described in chapter 12.

The sundisc takes on the meaning ascribed to it in chapters 12 and 14. The sundisc worn on the crown indicates that the individual is a living manifestation of the Central Sun energy and is therefore a servant of divine cosmic light and intelligence.

Tall double plumes of feathers. The feathered plumes are indicators of divine, universal truth worn with pride. The Truth Feather is discussed in chapter 14.

## The Cords of Completion

The Cords of Completion characterize eternal life. When initiates have achieved Ra-Harakhty (chapter 2), they are considered to be in an eternally ascending state of balance. This state can be equated with everlasting life since individuals are continually renewing themselves through *ka, ra, ptah,* and *phah*. Through Ra-Harakhty, they are continually re-creating (rather than destroying) themselves and can be considered to be experiencing perpetual ascension. Eternal life does not mean everlasting physical life but rather everlasting spiritual life.

At this point, Horus (the animation symbol of Ra-Harakhty) assigns the initiate the two Cords of Completion. The cords are symbolic of the connection to everlasting spiritual life because they run from the crown of the initiate (from the heavens) and into the Earth. The cords are grounded in the Earth, like lightning bolts, via the eternal soul–or Boreal (see chapter 16). The Bennu bird (Phoenix), which represents continual resurrection or eternal life, watches over this process and assists with spiritual grounding in the present, or physical, reality (see chapter 12, the Bennu bird).

Usually individuals who have achieved the Cords of

Completion are seen in glyphs kneeling between the two cords. The cords come out from the crown-chakra and descend directly into the Earth on each side of the initiate. Below is a slightly different version of this concept in which the student inscribes her will on a cord.

In this image from the Luxor Temple; the initiate inscribes one of their Cords of Completion. At the bottom of the cord is the Ben-Ben or Phoenix sitting on top of the Boreal.

At the top left of the image is the Sound ovoculum (see chapter 15), and above that is the wasp glyph grouping (see chapter 16).

## The Sacred Ibis Staff

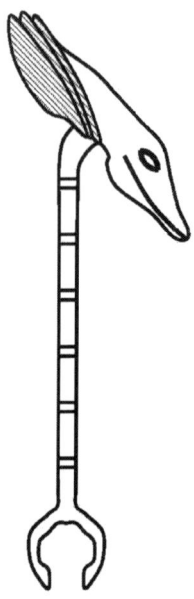

The sacred ibis staff (*ankhanet*) is awarded to high-priests and high-priestesses only. The sacred ibis is a large black and white bird with a long curved dark gray beak. The beak curves gently into the cheek, ending in an apparent smile. When flying overhead, the sacred ibis appears to be white, except for a thin line of black around the feather edge. This coloring represents the ultimate spiritual quest of the journey of life and the fact that the attainment of mastery contains infinite potential.

The sacred ibis always, and only, speaks the truth to whoever is prepared to listen. When this ibis appears in a person's life, she is ready for deep and lasting spiritual transformation. Life will slowly but surely begin to change for the individual who comes into intimate and unexpected contact with the sacred ibis. This ibis is ptah, or absolute service to life, and it speaks with the voice of the god-spirit.

The initiate who experiences an encounter with the sacred ibis, and who listens intently and carefully to the silent internal voice with which the bird speaks, must prepare for a life removed from the mainstream of society as well as increased isolation. The appearance of the sacred ibis does not mean loneliness. If initiates are willing and able to hear the truthful tales of this bird, then they are ready to fully embrace the constructs of their own souls. More often than not, this means that they will become increasingly separate from the distractions of conventional society and more committed to their dedicated soul paths. The sacred ibis can only appear in a person's life when the individual is free of fear, and open to the wondrous aspects of all life, especially the love that humanity is able to facilitate. The sacred ibis initiate will already have an excellent conception of who they are and why they are alive—in other words, it is likely that they would already have been initiated as a priest or priestess.

The appearance of the sacred ibis in an initiate's life will herald the time when they are ready to step even further up the ladder of consciousness and begin to teach all that they know to others. Whereas the ordinary priests and priestesses are mostly concerned with the intimate teachings of the Mysteries within the school system, high-priests and high-priestesses are able to channel knowledge from every aspect of universal life. In this way, high-priests and high-priestesses are not necessarily confined to the activities of the Mysterie Schools, although they know full well how to use what they have learnt in their spiritual training within the material world. The high-priests and high-priestesses are multidimensional beings, who are completely conscious of their fleeting presence within the human body in a worldly life. They are absolutely aware at every minute of the day how to manifest their divine purpose, but they are not rigidly bound to any personal ambition or calling. Those whose lives have been touched by the sacred ibis have officially taken up the call of the greater universe; they have become channels for what needs to be done at specific times and specific places to ensure that divine intelligence unfolds.

High-priests and high-priestesses are servants of cosmic creation and can hear, with absolute clarity, the requests of higher universal orders. Naturally, these individuals have reached an advanced level of spiritual development—so high, in fact, that they realize the futility of attempting to directly pass on their knowledge or wisdom to others. Their role of service and teaching is therefore more abstract; often, their best form of teaching is simply *being themselves*. The high-priests and high-priestesses remain eternally fluid in their activities; while they have an excellent grasp of the potentiality in future worldly events and the overall desires of universal forces, they also know that nothing is cast in stone, nothing is absolute, and that they must eternally adjust their thinking and doing to suit the organic unfolding of divine evolution. This state, which we call *per-mana* or simply *mana*, is the opposite of existentialism. The individual is fully conscious of the orderly, meaningful nature of the universe and acutely aware of, and grateful for, his role in it. This role might last a moment, a series of moments, a lifetime, or a series of lifetimes; no matter the earthly time allotted to his purpose, it is required to be fulfilled perfectly and in a timely manner, in accordance with the absolute rule of service we call *ptah*.

The high-priests and high-priestesses who have attained the ankhanet are continually provided with clear, precise cosmic knowledge and guidance to which they are able to listen and respond to with an open mind and a clear heart. These individuals live in a state of continual change, because the nature of divine intelligence is one of constantly unfolding evolution. The servants of the sacred ibis achieve security and peace in their understanding of themselves as divine godly instruments. They are intensely involved in developing life, but also powerfully separate; they are able to transcend the material world through their work. The individuals who have attained the sacred ibis staff are spiritual shape-shifters—not bound by physical constructs and mental concepts but absolutely true to the shifting nature of cosmic evolution.

This is an example of an initiate's experience of the sacred ibis:

*It was not long after I had experienced my initiation within the great pyramid that I noticed the birds continually flying over my rooms in the mornings and evenings. We are all familiar with the sacred ibis, but from below it looks very different, and I was not accustomed to the immensity of the birds that I kept seeing overhead. I could see where they were roosting, and this too was unusual, because it was not their natural habitat.*

*Not thinking of the birds, one day I took a stroll through the gardens at lunch hour. I paused for no particular reason at a bend in the path and, for no particular reason, looked up into a tall leafy tree above and before me. There, perched magically upon one of the branches, was a juvenile sacred ibis. Its feathers were mostly gray—it was still young and fluffy. But it was huge.*

*The long curving beak protruded powerfully from its small face. The beak ended in the cheek and turned upwards so that the creature seemed to be smiling. The bird watched me intensely. I watched the bird intensely.*

*For a while, we observed each other, until the bird began to speak to me in the deep, resonating voice of ptah—the natural voice of vital god-energy. Of course, the voice was not heard out loud, but I could feel the words echoing through my senses as clearly as if they were being read to me. It was amusing to hear such a deep, clear masculine voice coming from a dainty, feathered bird. The bird told me a number of things about the point in life I had reached and how events were unfolding for me. At that time, I was working with a group of intellectuals on some regional matters of our land, and I sometimes felt a little afloat and above it all—like I wasn't exactly sure where I was meant to be at what time and doing what. The bird assured me that I would always be at the right place at the right time. It also told me that I would shortly be experiencing swift and dramatic changes in my life that had been carefully planned and were anticipated.*

*After a bit more chit-chat, the sacred ibis lifted off the branch and flew directly over my head so that I could see the underside of its belly and the black-trimmed whiteness of its feather array. Thank you, ibis.*

The sacred ibis staff may be granted to a high-priest or high-priestess who ironically may no longer be part of the Mysterie School system. The ankhanet represents that they have passed through the spiritual lessons of the schools to the highest level possible and have transcended the need to be confined to any human societal system. The sacred ibis head at the top of the staff symbolizes that the individual who carries the staff always speaks, listens, and acts in accordance with divine truth and the cosmic plan. Carriers of the ankhanet, which means *life in motion*, are thoroughly aware of their purposes in life but are also always ready to make adjustments to suit ptah.

The shaft of the ankhanet is ribbed and at its base is carved the open prong of the tuning fork. This staff is not only symbolic of a spiritual soothsayer, but it may also be used to test energetically the existence of truth in a person or situation. When our spiritual brethren were at their strongest, a high-priest or high-priestess in possession of the ankhanet was able to command the floor at any gathering or meeting—voices would simply cease when the holder had a viewpoint to share, since it was understood that he or she was a channel for divine, absolute universal truth.

Since Thoth the ibis is the representative of sacred truth, the ankhanet is also a symbol of Thoth. They are one and the same. See chapter 12, Thoth.

## Statues

We like to display statues to remind the students why they are within the schools and who they really are. Many of our statues include the representations of initiations passed as described in this chapter. Also, we often sculpt a student who is either flanked by others or who has a much smaller version of an individual between his or her legs. Sometimes we portray three students in a row wearing evidence of initiations passed, such as various crowns.

The figures that flank the main students, or rest in miniature between their legs, are often considered to be guides for their higher-selves or parallel versions of themselves. Accompanying female statues may represent the feminine half of the individual or his or her twin energy flame. The head-dresses often alternate to show how each initiate is all of these things at once and how what appears to the world in the physical body is only a pale reflection of the true attainments of the spiritual body through the Mysterie School lessons.

Although the statues do not technically represent any initiation passed, they do serve to remind the students that their earthly bodies are merely vessels for their higher-selves, which is the part of them that remains eternally present on the ethereal planes and guides their physical bodies towards the activities that result in the highest good of all. It also reminds the students that they are part of a spiritual family and are always guided from the spiritual realm and are never alone. Within the schools, they are continually amongst like-minded individuals who aspire to the same heights. The left foot of the student is often forward to represent the heart-connection.

# Representations of Initiations Passed

A statue at Karnak Temple with an initiate in the pleated skirt, *nemset* head-dress, upper and lower crowns, chin-strap, diadem, and carrying the staff and flail. This could be the higher-self of the actual initiate who rests between the legs of the true spiritual and giant (larger-than-life) version of himself or herself.

# 12

## Egypt and Egyptian Gods

The land now called Egypt was the holy crypt of the Sun God energy for a long time. The Sun God energy is the creative source or power that fuels our universe. The primary home of the Sun God(s) is the Great Central Sun, which forms the centrifugal point of the universal system. The Great Central Sun is more than a manifested solar energy—it is like a cosmic sun that emits spiritual light only. Spiritual light is soft, ethereal light that penetrates every corner of space. The smaller, physical suns scattered across the heavens—such as the sun around which the Earth moves—are micro-manifestations of the Great Central Sun. These smaller suns are children of the Great Central Sun, but they do not emit the same intensity of spiritual light. The obelisk is the symbol of the Sun God energy.

The Sun God energy has been responsible for the creation of much life in our universe and was partly responsible for the creation of humankind. Most important, it is the light emitted by this god-energy that sustains all life, either directly or indirectly within our universe. Therefore, the sundisc is venerated within our Mystical Schools because we consider it the source of all-that-is. The Sun God energy may exist at any time in any part of the universe that it desires—in fact, it will osmose into any vessel that is sufficiently open to accept the blessing of its beneficent light.

When our ancestors were led to the land of Egypt after Atlantis disappeared, they christened it Iyrgr, which means New Earth. The significance of Iyrgr is that it exists at the sacred point where the primary vertical and horizontal ley-lines of your planet meet. Ley-lines are lines of intense energy that are created on the Earth's surface from the electromagnetic waves of the rays of the Great Central Sun. Egypt held the balance of energies on Earth for many thousands of years; but when Egypt fell, those energies spread to the entire planet, mostly into shifting pockets of consciousness.

As a result of the presence and role of the Sun God energy within earthly life, solar symbols are very prolific within the Mysteries. You will also be familiar with Akhenaton's Aten in this respect. Akhenaton, a dedicated disciple of the Mysteries, diligently endeavored to resurrect our beliefs during his time. But he was working more than 1,500 years after our golden age ended and against a tide of human ignorance and stubbornness; it was difficult for him.

It is our belief that the initiates who become pharaohs are direct servants of the Sun God energy, assisting in the perpetuation of divine love and life through their very being. They become manifested forms of the Sun Gods.

Many of the creations that are now referred to as Egyptian gods are either literal, or figurative, conceptions of the Sun Gods. For example, the Hathors are an extraterrestrial race created by the Sun Gods, but Thoth is a universal concept that serves the overall Sun God. Thoth is neither an entity nor a god-energy. Another example is Amun, which means light, and is not a god at all. Most of the entities in the cosmic pantheon that you may understand as Egyptians gods, are merely representations of universal concepts, words or terms from the Mysteries, or energies and beings that assist in universal order.

The concepts referred to as Re, Ay, Shu, and Ney are discussed in chapter 4, *The Sacred Elementals*, although Re is discussed further below.

Here we provide a brief glossary of the Egyptian gods:

**Amon:** Amon is not a god-energy; it means *silence* or more precisely *absence of sound*. Amon is often associated with Mut (stillness) and Khons (focus/concentration).

**Amun-Ra:** Amun means light, specifically cosmic spiritual light, and ra means the relational connection to others. When ra is used in combination with other words, such as Amun, it takes on a slightly different, more figurative, meaning. Ra in this instance means a connection to all things and consequently to the pathways leading to all things. Within this context, ra describes the connection to source-energy, or the Source itself.

Amun-Ra therefore means Light-Source.

**Anubis:** Anubis, the jackal-headed god, is the universal guardian of sacred places and experiences. Since the most mystical experiences usually occur in sleep or trans-meditation, Anubis has been associated with the subconscious or with figurative death.

Anubis holds the power of the universe until an individual is ready to facilitate this spiritual power on Anubis' behalf. The jackal god will then transfer universal power to the individual who is ready to experience evolution through enlightenment.

The staff of Anubis represents the delegated universal power that a priest or priestess may use in their role as spiritual leader and teacher. The staff is shown in chapter 14.

Anubis is also known as the Protector of Pathways.

**Aten:** The Aten, identified with the sun or the sundisc is the very essence of our universe. From it all life has been born, and to it all life will return. It is the constant energy that can never die or fade—only transmute. In this instance, the sun is more than one of the physical burning bodies that we call suns or stars; it is the ever-present energy or life-force omnipresent in the universe; it can also be called the Great Central Sun. It gives life, it is life—and therefore it is the essence of humankind. The stellar suns that we observe are merely physical manifestations of this life-force energy. Humankind's connection to the sun is invisible, but as the disc rises and sets each day it reminds us of all-that-is and of the miracle of being alive.

**Atum:** Atum is a direct translation of *humankind* and is not a god-energy.

**Baboon:** Where the baboon appears, either as a figure or head-dress, there is a suggestion of the mastery of time. The baboon represents the phases of the moon and guards the cycles of time on the Earth-plane. Overcoming the illusory limitations of time in physical reality means that an individual has attained the wisdom of the baboon.

Chapter 16 provides an example of our annual calendar.

**Bennu:** This bird, often called the Ben-Ben and identified with the phoenix, embodies everlasting life or spiritual resurrection. The phoenix was a bird that existed in our time and had an unusual method of shedding its feathers. The baby Ben-Bens are a plain gray when born. Upon reaching adulthood the feathers become a brilliant white that reflects sunlight so strongly they appear to be on fire. Thereafter, the bird loses all of its feathers and becomes bald. The feathers that grow back are a multifarious mixture of yellows, reds, and oranges—like flames of the sun.

The Ben-Ben reminds us that from mundane, human life can come the brilliance of a life lived in cosmic illumination. The phoenix is mentioned in chapter 11, Cords of Completion.

**Hathor:** The Hathors are the intergalactic cousins of human beings. They are extraterrestrials who are great friends of the Earth and have been involved in her evolution since the human race began. The Hathors initiated the teachings of the Mysteries in Egypt, in tandem with our ancestors from Atlantis.

**Horus:** Horus, the Hawk or Falcon, is the animation symbol for Ra-Harakhty (see Ra-Harakhty later in this section).

Above is a stone engraving of Horus in anthropomorphic form, crowned with the cobra encircling the sundisc. See chapter 16 for a glyph of the head of Horus, as well as an explanation of the cobra and sundisc.

Horus shows how the individual, and therefore humanity at large, is capable of attaining great spiritual heights by following a path of inner truth. In essence, personal truth is universal truth. From Horus' higher perspective, where he glides through the skies, he guides the soul to fulfilling its purpose and achieving spiritual clarity. Horus is a cosmic bird that facilitates spiritual growth towards attainment of a permanent union of the soul with that of the god-energy or all-that-is. Horus leads the soul towards illumination.

In trans-meditation, the hawk carries the *ba*, or astral body, to the non-physical plane (see chapter 9). Another symbol of Horus is the Eye of Horus or the All-Seeing Eye (chapter 16).

**Isis:** Isis means *life;* since life is a process of love in freedom of expression, Isis may also represent love.

The direct translation of Isis is closest to "release" or "freedom." Isis reminds us that our souls are always free to escape the confines of the human body and ego if we desire. Ultimately, we are all part of the same evolving universe, and our souls can never truly be separated from the omnipotent and omnipresent love that fuels the stars and all other things in the cosmos. Therefore, Isis is often associated with the Love ovoculum as well as the winged initiate who may reach the heavens via trans-meditation, and join the Great Sky Vulture (see Nekhabet below). The vulture's wingspan shows the presence and potential of Isis. The wings can be seen extending from below the arms of initiates—either with arms outstretched, or wrapped around the body.

The animation symbol for Isis is a three-scale xylophone of the musical scales *g, f,* and *d* (see chapter 8 and 16).

Isis is the concept of life and is generally understood as the female archetype, paired with Osiris (service to life) as the male archetype (see Osiris in this section).

Love and Light are considered the two pillars of wisdom (see ovocula, chapter 15). Isis often accompanies the Love ovoculum and Nephthys (a symbol of light) often accompanies the Light ovoculum; therefore, Isis and Nephthys frequently appear together.

See Nephthys in this section. The combined animation symbols appear in chapter 16.

**Khephri:** This is the scarab, also referred to as Khepru or Kephren. These names all loosely mean *keeper* or *carrier*. The scarab is a carrier of light and the sundisc or Aten.

Chapter 14 describes the scarab.

**Khnum or the Ram God:** Khnum is the energy responsible for all ruminants on planet Earth. For example, Khnum oversees the birth, death, and life of goats, sheep, cows, and buck. The Ram god energy exists in the pure white light of love, and Khnum richly rewards those humans who serve and protect his animals.

Khnum energy is another servant of the Sun God and therefore often animates our statuettes and sphinxes. The ram energy is primarily a masculine one.

**Khons:** Khons is not a god-energy but a concept, meaning *focus* or *concentration*, specifically with reference to spiritual studies or meditation.

Therefore Khons is often mentioned with Amon (silence), and Mut (or stillness).

**Mayet:** Mayet is not a god-energy but a derivative of *mana*—the shape-shifting state recognized by the Sacred Ibis Staff or *ankhanet*. It is therefore associated with truth. The Sacred Ibis Staff is discussed in chapter 11.

**Memnon:** Memnon is the snake god, and servant of the Sun God. Memnon is often represented (upright) as a cobra with the sundisc above its hood—the Uraeus symbol. When initiates are depicted in art or glyph with a crown of snakes and suns, it means that the individuals are perfect channels for the will of god. They are columns of oneness with the everlasting god-energy and true servants of the light.

Although the human heart has four physical chambers, it has six metaphysical ones. These six chambers are the engine of the human system, each playing a role in giving power to human life. From a scientific point of view, the brain is responsible for governing all awake-state behavior, but it is the human heart that is the real generator of three-dimensional life; it is from the heart-center that the divine self and the material self come together to perform the miracles of human life. See Life Throne, chapter 14.

The snake god, Memnon, reminds us of human potential as he spreads his hood to reveal the six chambers painted with the primary colors of blue, red, and green.

Memnon is lord of the physical Earth or that which lies below.

See Nekhabet, the god of upper life.

**Mut:** Mut is not a god-energy but a concept meaning *stillness*; it is often associated with Amon (silence) and Khons (focus/concentration).

**Neith:** Neith is not a god-energy; her name means initiate or neophyte.

**Nekhabet, the Great Sky Vulture:** When the Earth began, Nekhabet (the Great Sky Vulture) spread itself across the sky in order to protect the planet and all of its life. At night when you look up, you will observe the shape of the vulture in the star pattern that is now known as the Milky Way. However, the star arm that extends across the heavens around the Earth is Nekhabet, which can loosely be translated as "protector" or "nurturer".

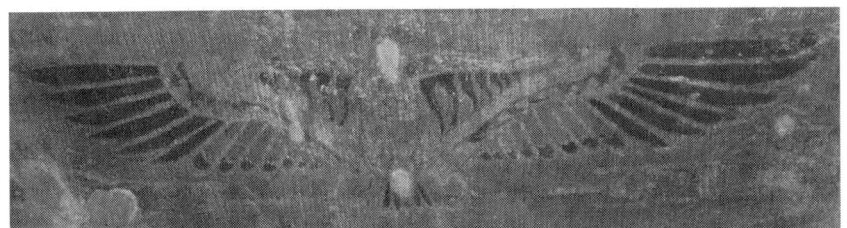

The image above shows the Sky Vulture on the roof of a temple. A stylized image of the vulture is also given in chapter 16.

Humankind was created in the image of the heavens and therefore in the image of the Sun God, the centrifugal energy that fuels our universe. Within the galaxy in which humankind exists, the father vulture watches over all. At all times, the great expanse of his wings stretches across the heavens and at night the stars bring his form alive. He intently looks down at the creation and watches life as it unfolds on Earth. He knows the whole past, present, and future; he reminds human beings to live up to their unlimited and constantly evolving potential. The vulture is also a creation of the Sun God and has been sent as the Watcher.

The vulture is often seen in glyphs carrying the boreal symbol, the flattened ankh that signifies everlasting spiritual life (see chapter 16). The Great Sky Vulture is a carrier, protector, and nurturer of all spiritual life—and therefore all human souls as well as the great eternal soul that permeates all living manifestations.

Nekhabet is lord of the upper spiritual world or that which lies above. Connecting with the Sky Vulture is described in the discussion on trans-mediation, chapter 9.

See Memnon, the god of earthly life.

**Nephthys (Nebet-Het):** In direct translation, Nephthys means transformational unfoldment. It can also be equated with spiritual evolution. The cosmic light contains all colors of the rainbow and so forms a perfect blend of luminescent white. Human beings are miniature versions of this cosmic light and have been endowed with the power to shine like multifarious rainbows within their earthly life. As spiritual evolution increases so does this divine luminescence. Nephthys often accompanies the Light ovoculum and is closely associated with the lotus flower, which is the animation symbol of spiritual illumination or opening (discussed in chapters 13 and 16).

The animation symbol for Nephthys is the singing bowl. When the seven musical notes corresponding to the seven colors of the rainbow are emitted from the singing bowl in ascending order, the sound waves (if visible) open like a lotus flower to the sun. The sound waves circle the bowl in ever-widening rings until a constant vibration emanates from the bowl like a quivering lotus of light. See chapter 16, the symbol for Nephthys.

Light and Love are considered the two pillars of wisdom (see chapter 15, ovocula). Nephthys often accompanies the Light ovoculum, and Isis often accompanies the Love ovoculum; therefore Nephthys and Isis frequently appear together.

See Isis above. These combined animation symbols appear in chapter 16.

**Nut:** Nut is a reference to the sky and the Shu element (See chapter 4, The Sacred Elements). Nut often refers to the sky goddess and is an important image associated with trans-meditation.

**Osiris:** Like Isis, Osiris takes many forms and figures. Essentially, Osiris means *service to life*, which can also be broadly interpreted as god-is-all; therefore, all life is lived through service to god.

This great all-encompassing concept of Osiris permeates many aspects of the Mysteries. Since Isis means *life* (the more feminine principle) and Osiris means *service to life* (the more masculine principle), Isis and Osiris are often depicted together. Like Ptah, Osiris is frequently seen shrouded in white cloth, meaning the relinquishment of the individual ego to divine order and humility. Osiris and Ptah share many similarities; the subtle difference is that while Ptah oversees daily service to life and humanity within Ra-Harakhty (a moment-to-moment energy), Osiris is the cosmic embodiment of service to all life (a universal energy that fuels evolution).

Osiris may hold the ankhanet (ibis scepter)—or a collection of scepters, including an ankh, flail, staff, and Djed-pillar. The meanings of these various symbols are explained in chapters 3, 11, and 14.

The All-Seeing Eye (Eye of Horus) is the animation symbol for Osiris, explained in chapter 16.

The Sirius and Orion portals of the fixed stars are the gateways through which the universal masters of Osiris operate and from where the name Osiris derives. These cosmic bodies are not stars or planets but intergalactic portals that permanently emit a tremendous light and a hypo-magnetic flux, as explained in chapter 6. The portals are an instantaneous gateway to other parts of the universe, including other time-realities. The universal beings who have mastered the Osirian energy, and actively assist with the evolution of planet Earth (with service to life), enter and exit our galaxy via these portals.

**Ptah:** Ptah is the attainment of service to all of humanity and all of life (see chapter 2). Ptah is usually represented in a white mummified form with a black or blue skullcap. The binding of the cloth around Ptah represents the relinquishment of the human ego to the work of the divine, and the skullcap symbolizes absolute humility in service and absence of vanity. Alternatively, Ptah may be wrapped in Isis wings (see Isis in this section).

Like Osiris, Ptah may hold the ankhanet, because those who have achieved ptah speak with absolute truth in their role of service to universal life. Alternatively, Ptah (like Osiris) can hold a collection of scepters including an ankh, flail, staff, and Djed-pillar. The meanings of these various symbols are explained in chapters 3, 11, and 14. The blue of the skullcap is synchronous with the color of the fifth energy chakra of truth.

In stone or illustrated reliefs, an individual may often be seen embracing or close to Ptah, in a divine act of surrender to living service.

Ptah is the cosmic brother of Osiris, who is also an emblem of universal service to life (see Osiris in this section).

**Ra-Harakhty (Ra-Horakhty):** This is the collective mystical name for the Four Teachers of Life that lead an initiate towards self-mastery: *ka, ra, ptah,* and *phah* (see chapter 2). The animation symbol for Ra-Harakhty is Horus the falcon/hawk. (See Horus in this section.) The achievement of Ra-Harakhty is required for Level 4 of the schooling—or *phara*-ship.

**Re:** This is not a god-energy but is one of the four sacred elementals of the cosmos. It is the element associated with fire, sun/sunlight, gold metal, and cosmic spiritual light (Amun), amongst others. See chapter 4.

**Sekhmet (Sakhmet):** Sekhmet is another servant of the Sun God energy. She appears in the form of a lion; quite often a white lion. She is the overseer of divine order sent to rectify the wrongs of the world, assisting humanity in recognizing themselves and their role in cosmic evolution. Sekhmet is a ruthless envoy for universal peace who stops at nothing to bring order and love out of chaos and fear. The lion energy of the Sun God works through the cat kingdom, somewhat surreptitiously but ever-present. Wherever the lion appears, as in the image of the sphinxes, what you understand as Christ Consciousness is taking form.

**Selket:** Selket (also called Selkit and Serket) is not a god-energy, but means Scorpio—as in the constellation and astrological symbol.

**Tefenet:** Sometimes referred to as Tefnut, Tefenet is a combination of the ney and shu elements of water (net) and sky (nut), such as for dew and rain. See chapter 4 for more on the manifestations of shu and ney.

**Thoth:** Thoth, the Ibis-headed god, means divine truth in manifestation, such as through speech, writing, thought, deeds, and other forms of communication and being. Thoth guards the portal to the Akashic universal temple, in which all truth of cosmic life and individual souls is carefully recorded, arranged, and protected.

The animation symbol for Thoth is the ibis. The strong, long curved beak of the bird represents the channel through which divine truth may be facilitated. The beak extends far into the small face of the ibis and appears to end in a smile at the cheek. The curved smile of the beak takes up much of the face of the bird, and metaphorically encapsulates the eye and the brain of the creature—indicating how thought, speech, observation, and general communication and intelligence are all part of the same function. The Ibis shows how divine truth should regulate one's thinking, speaking, seeing, writing, doing and any other manifestations of animated life.

The priests/priestesses are a link to the universe and universal masters. They are not more special than the rest of humankind, but they have perfected the art of divine communication. The scribe god, Thoth, assists the pharaohs with the translation of divine universal lore into everyday life. It is no mystery, but it requires an open heart. Thoth works specifically through written truth *(kathar/thar)*. Kathar/thar is a manifestation of truth that transcends all universal language.

The sacred ibis staff *(ankhanet)* indicates that the individual who carries the staff always speaks, listens, and acts in accordance with divine truth and the cosmic plan. The ankhanet is explained in chapter 11.

# 13

## Attaining Illumination

Our guess is that you skipped directly to this chapter. Let us say this once and clearly so that you can go back to the beginning of the book: no person or thing can tell you who you really are, why you are alive, or what you are meant to be doing in life.

The realization and acceptance of this fact is what illumination is. Once you have discovered these things for *yourself*, the old way of life where only obstacles existed will fall away, and you will be born into a new way of life—you will be born into yourself.

In life, you meet many people, situations, and things that may or may not point you in the right direction—the right direction being the direction in which the soul wants to travel. At some point, you learn to recognize good advice and legitimate signposts. But at no time—and we repeat, *at no time*—are you given explicit, detailed information on the soul's true desire and the exact path you must follow to attain that destiny. This is true within the Mysteries as well. The schools and the spiritual lessons are designed to emulate life. Therefore, while we do everything to facilitate the attainment of illumination for our students, and guide them towards their own truth, we cannot guarantee or ensure that they will attain illumination at any point. That choice is theirs.

The reason for this limited interference by cosmic forces in human life is simple. *You are your own great creative work.* True artists do not paint by numbers, or sketch the work of others, or allow others to constantly whisper direction in their ears. They create from their souls and from their heart, working diligently until a masterpiece begins to unfold; in that unfoldment, they are given a clearer and clearer image of what the result might be. Your destiny unfolds as you desire it, it changes as you change it, and the result is yours—uniquely yours.

This seems simple, but the greatest difficulty in life is being able to differentiate the desire of the ego from that of the soul or higher-self. Learning the difference between the false baggage of the ego trip and the true integrity of the soul's choice is where mastery is achieved. There is a difference between consciousness and illumination. Human beings can be spiritually conscious while simultaneously grappling with the material precepts of life. Mastery coupled with consciousness produces illumination. However, mastery is not a finite thing. The belief that attaining mastery is absolute and final is a limiting one; it trips up many students. As humans, it is possible to experience mastery in one moment and to feel separated from it in the next. When a person can maintain a state of mastery from moment-to-moment—despite the events unfolding in his life—he has achieved lasting mastery or what we call illumination.

Illumination does not mean that a person's life becomes perfect in the short-term; on the contrary, she may become increasingly challenged by responsibilities and trials. Illumination means that she is closer to finding her own everlasting peace, either in this life or in another.

The premise of our school system is that we prepare souls for

# Attaining Illumination

higher states of being—we are working with the *spiritual selves* of the students. It is far too simplistic to say that the condition of a person's external life is a reflection of their internal world, because a myriad of controllable and uncontrollable factors influence an individual's day-to-day life. Therefore, at the schools, we work on the core of our student, which is the invisible spiritual body. We endeavor to prepare the student for evermore perfect states of existence, both within the material world and in the ethereal realms.

Seeking higher states of consciousness is a timeless process—it is evolution itself. Therefore, we never push or control our initiates. As priests and priestesses of the Mysterie Schools, we are obliged to stand back, and in accordance with divine life allow them to make their own decisions. Their mistakes are as painful to them as they are to us; we know that they eventually will begin to make the right decisions. The teachings of the schools provide a beautiful foundation for exquisite, illuminated life, and serve the student well into future incarnations. There are many of our initiates alive today who are still following the path of spiritual mastery that we set their souls on many thousands of years ago in Egypt. It is wonderful to watch from our perspective.

⬇

In chapter 2 we explained how reaching illumination is analogous to reaching the apex of a pyramid. The miracle of illumination is that the top of the pyramid is not an end—it is more like a beginning—since realization explodes out from the apex and spreads in every direction, like rays of light expanding from a sun. Upon illumination, there is a knowingness of the self and therefore of divine universal intelligence, which means the individual is familiar with the unlimited potential of all-that-is. When initiates are illuminated, they know that the top of the pyramid doesn't so much continue to expand upwards as it spreads to infinity in every direction. This can be equated to a plateau of understanding (*nevana*), absolute mastery, illumination, or full consciousness.

It is difficult for us to explain how the state of illumination feels; it needs to be experienced. It is impossible to describe the experience of joining the divine universal order through spiritual ascension. Once you are on the plateau of understanding, you will realize the futility of pressurizing others to follow the same path up the light-pyramid. There is really only one path of illumination open to every soul, and that is the path of self-choosing or self-discovery.

The 7th Level of the Mysterie School includes a ritual within one of the great pyramids, the vehicle being trans-meditation. This ritual seeks to initiate the individual into the universal order. At this point, the initiates cease to be students of the school system, because they have become students of a greater, more powerful school—the universal school of life. In your modern era, human beings are born directly into this school of life, even though many crave the spiritual insight and order produced by the Mysterie Schools of the past. We encourage those of you who feel that huge aspects of spiritual life are missing from the modern world to keep looking for solutions. Many movements, orders, and organizations on your planet are perpetuating the lessons of the Mysterie Schools. The way of the Mysteries is not for everybody; for others, it is a necessity. Some of you alive today are destined for spiritual mastery and leadership—you crave mystical knowledge like others crave food.

A person who has been initiated into the universal order of spiritual mastery (Level 7) may not have attained ultimate illumination; however, he cannot retrogress. If he does not achieve illumination in the particular life in which he completed his mundane spiritual lessons, he will return again and again into life until illumination is achieved. This is not a punishment. It is like a child beginning a series of new paintings until he is content with the result. Illumination is a personal choice and a personal journey. Once any lesson has been learnt at a soul level, it is learnt forever. The Mysterie Schools place great emphasis on spiritual mastery because it is a state that transcends material, ephemeral life—either on the Earth or in some other place. Soul lessons are part of everlasting spiritual life and are part of each soul's personal imprint forever.

One of our favorite analogies for illumination is that of the lotus lily. The seed of the lotus germinates in the mud of a pond. When the seed begins to sprout, it will grow out of the mud and into the murky water. Emerging from the mud is not the end of its journey; although the water is easier to grow through than the mud, it is still murky. The stem will grow through the water for a while until it bursts into the air. Life in the open air is so much nicer than the water, but it is still not the end. Leaves may grow from the stem—and then a flower. But the flower is still not the end. The flower can open and unfold with the rays of the sun shining from above.

In this analogy, we encounter the four elements: earth (ay), water (ney), air (shu), and sunlight (re). The growth of the lotus is like the growth of a soul towards illumination. At each stage in which the soul moves from one element to another (or from one stage of consciousness to another), its perspective on life becomes less murky. If it persists, there will come a time when it can unfold its spiritual petals fully to the light of cosmic consciousness and absorb all the delicious rewards of an illuminated life.

⁌

All the lessons and steps of the Mysterie Schools—or of life itself—are designed to bring us closer to the absolute secret of the universe. That secret is ourselves.

Therefore, the schools only facilitate the journey towards the self—they cannot explain it or replace it. One of the miracles of life is that every life-form is a microcosm or a macrocosm of some other part of life. Human beings are like miniature solar systems. The heart-center, which is like the Great Central Sun, is surrounded by a series of colorful energy centers (chakras), which are like planets surrounding the centrifugal heart. As tiny as the physical human body is within the immensity of our universe, the human spirit is as powerful as any solar system or even the universe at large. The god-energy permeates all parts of life; humanity is as god-like as anything that exists in our ever-evolving all-that-is.

Therefore, to know the self, is to know god. This, really, is the great mystery of the Mysterie Schools—the great mystery of life. It is so easy to become distracted in the everyday chaos of life on Earth and to allow the ego to take you on endless deviations away from your true path. But returning to the path, you return to yourself, and you return to god and the promise of everlasting peace. It is when you stop fighting yourself and your own nature that the eternal peace and grace of the god-energy can find a home in you, and you a home in it.

Thoth is a reminder of this fact. As he guards the portal to Akasha—the timeless records of who you are and have ever been—he silently whispers a fervent prayer: Know thyself. Because it is only through knowing yourself that you know all and are initiated into the universal order of divine intelligence and everlasting peace.

Sometimes Thoth stands on either side of a pair of false doors. The frame of the doors is made of stone and is so strong that we imagine what lies inside must be tremendous, and it is. As Thoth slides the doors open and releases the four winds of eternity into the world, we are able to get a glimpse of the vision that he unleashes. As the Thoths move to the left and right, they shift the past back, and the future forward, to reveal the present. The present moment is a mirror that shows us the tremendous power of the self through which human beings are able to conduct the will of god—the will of themselves. To do this, they must first recognize themselves, know themselves, and accept themselves. They must accept their power.

**A set of false doors of stone**

We will end with one of the meditations that we use to get the students into trans-meditation. This meditation draws on the promise made by Thoth.

*You are flying down a valley. The valley is green and quiet, and hills roll in from each side in alternating gentle waves. You are flying straight forward and are above the Earth's surface. Below you in the valley is a beautiful, clear river of glistening blue. The wind pushes quickly past your face and cools the skin that has warmed from your beating heart. You can smell the trees, the grass, the air, the flowers, and the water of the river that rushes down the valley below you. You can hear the wind, the birds, the water, and the swish of grass as you fly deeper and deeper into the valley. You can see the long line of river that stretches out below you, the swaying of trees and grass, and the shadows of the clouds on the Earth. You can feel the pulse of your heart as you race up the valley—and the wind rushing against your skin. Although you cannot see them, you suspect you have a great pair of wings that propel you forward through the valley. You are flying faster and faster towards some destination as the green hills roll away to your left and right.*

*You drop lower and closer to the water so that you can hear its rush. You are following this rush upstream to the source of its power. Ahead of you, you discern a waterfall at the end of the valley. You continue to fly faster and faster to this wall of water. The waterfall draws closer and closer. You fly faster and faster. The waterfall gets closer. The images to the left and right are now blurred, and you are completely focused on the picture ahead. You slow down as the waterfall appears before you. You get as close as you can to the glistening, rushing water, until you feel the heavy spray on your skin and are deafened by the roar of the fall. You hover at the face of the waterfall—well above the ground—and observe how the sunlight reflects off the spray. The water is falling in tremendous torrents, but the sunlight appears still. You notice a beautiful reflection in the water, like an Angel staring back at you from another place. As the sun glints off the water, a myriad of drops continue to tumble in contented abandonment down the waterfall. That image you see in the waterfall—look at that image. What is it that you see?*

# 14
## High-Alphabet Glyphs

Although the high-alphabet (also called the feeling-alphabet) is far more simplistic and limited than the common or literary alphabet, its glyphs are based on universal concepts. Chapter 5 provided an introduction to the high-alphabet. In the next three chapters, we will show you some of the main hieroglyphs and glyph groupings that you will find within the Mysterie Schools.

Some of these individual glyphs, such as the Eye of Horus, are universal and timeless; some of the glyphs, such as the hibiscus flower, were drawn from the environs of our land at the time. However, the overall meanings of the glyphs of the high-alphabet relate to infinite, cosmic concepts.

Some hieroglyphs, such as the scarab, appear identical when the image is reversed. Other glyphs, like the golden staff, may face the left or the right. Technically there is no difference in the meaning of the glyph if it faces the left or the right, although a subtle emphasis is ascribed to the left as being more feminine and the right as being more masculine. This makes no difference to the feeling interpretation of the overall glyph or glyph grouping, however.

All glyphs have an independent meaning, although many high-alphabet glyphs are designed to appear in glyph groupings (chapter 16) or in ovocula (see below and chapter 15).

These examples are by no means exhaustive, but they provide

essential insight into our high-alphabet without undue complexity or detail. In most instances we have provided the pictograms, but for others you will need to use your imagination.

## Ovoculum

The ovoculum (plural: ovocula) is an oblong circlet that encompasses groups of glyphs of a sacred word or concept. The ovocula may appear horizontally or vertically, and the positions of the glyphs can be reversed, but they are always read from the knot at the base of the circlet.

Ovocula were never intended to be used for proper names within our system. Originally, proper names were inscribed within vertical rectangular blocks as part of the common alphabet. The ovocula shape was eventually adopted, erroneously in our view, to represent the names of kings who ruled after the golden age of the Mysteries.

All glyph groupings appearing within ovocula are part of the seven sacred concepts of the high-alphabet; for example, the concepts of Love and Light. The circlet represents the omnipresence of the concepts, despite being contained within a two-dimensional space as a set of glyphs. These are universal concepts that extend above and beyond human life on Earth. They are transcendental, omnipotent concepts.

The line below or to the side of the circlet, and the knot that binds the line to the circlet, represent the solidification of these terms within physical life. Altogether, the ovoculum looks like a mirror in which the sacred concepts may be reflected by humanity in their life journeys.

For example, using a group of six hieroglyphs:

# High-Alphabet Glyphs

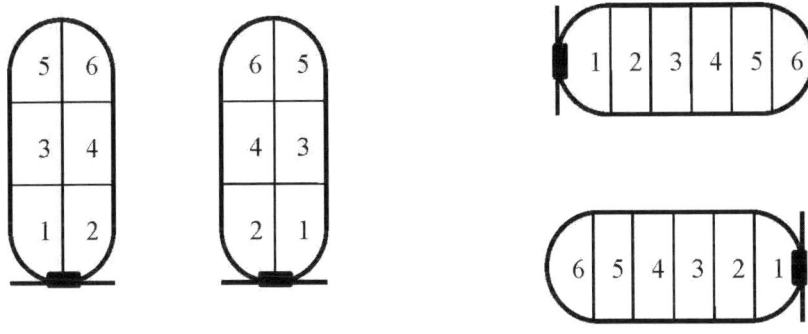

Refer to chapter 15 for an expansion on the seven sacred ovocula of the high-alphabet.

## Sun (Sundisc)
*The Source / source-energy / all-that-is / the Aten*

The sundisc is a symbol of the manifested Sun God energy that is explained in the introduction and Aten section of chapter 12. This symbol may also be referred to as the Aten, because in this hieroglyphic form, the sundisc is representative of much more than the physical sun; it is the spiritual manifestation of source-energy that powers the universe.

When the sundisc appears in a glyph grouping, it often emphasizes the omnipresence of that thing. For instance, when appearing with the Love ovoculum (chapter 15), it refers to all-encompassing love or absolute love. Any glyph that is crowned by the sundisc is considered to be operating as one with the Source—in divine accordance with all-that-is.

## Scarab Beetle
*The light-bringer / light-bearer / or light-carrier*

The scarab beetle is believed to be an incarnation of pure solar energy, which is evident when it tucks in its appendages and the body appears as a disc-like structure. The scarab may also be seen rolling balls of dung into which it lays its eggs. The balls provide all the nourishment the young need when they hatch. This is metaphorical of the sun or sundisc (all-that-is), because the sundisc is all-encompassing and provides humanity with everything it needs. As the scarab, or dung beetle, rolls its dung ball before it, it is as if the creature were carrying a source of life—or a sun.

The scarab beetle may take on slight variations, such as the acquisition of a pair of vulture's wings. The variations add a deeper dimension or meaning to the scarab; for example, the vulture's wings add a connotation of *all-encompassing* (explained in chapter 16). However, the essential meaning of the scarab beetle remains the same.

## Three Rods
*The third-dimensional reality of physical space / living manifestation*

When the three rods appear in a glyph combination, they are grounding the concept of the glyph in physical life. For example, in chapter 15, the Love ovoculum contains three rods above the inverted half-circle (see below). This means that the concept of the glyph grouping is being given structure in physical reality.

The glyph meaning is being brought down to Earth, into third-dimensional space.

## Half-circle (inverted)
*Carrier-of / home to / gives a place to live/manifest*

The inverted half-circle is one half of a sphere and reminiscent of one half of a sundisc. When this half-circle appears in a glyph grouping it indicates an open vessel or foundation upon which life can manifest. For instance, the planet Earth is a place or a vessel that has been provided for the evolution of conscious life-forms.

When the half-circle appears with other glyphs (such as the three rods above) the concept of manifested life in three-dimensional reality is reinforced.

## Bowl (or Basket)
*Provides / serves / serves as an instrument of*

The bowl is more elongated than the half circle and is often accompanied by two horizontal lines below, meaning *in the service of / in service to*. The horizontal lines indicate active motion (like a verb) and that something is being done or performed—in this case service.

Sometimes three small dashes appear below the horizontal lines. These dashes emphasize that the action of service is manifested in life or in physical reality.

A slight variation on this same concept is the bowl underscored by the three vertical rods lying next to shortened versions of the two horizontal bars.

## Eggshell
*Birth / awakening / new*

The eggshell is smaller than both the half-circle and the bowl. It is half an eggshell, indicating the egg has been cracked open. The eggshell is not an independent glyph and generally accompanies a glyph grouping. See the Quail Chick later in this section.

## Hibiscus Flower
*The color red / open / receptive*

When viewed from a side profile, the stamen of the blossoming hibiscus is a prominent extension of the flower. The sticky stamen forms the center of the open flower and is ready for pollen.

Although hibiscus flowers can be a variety of colors, they are often red.

## Flower of the Bulrush
*The color orange*

Although the bulrush may appear orange-brown in nature, it is most often rendered as orange.

## Golden Staff/Crook
*The color yellow / service / humility*

The staff is the symbol of lifelong service in humility to love and light. When a student is presented with a staff, it will be carved from gold. The staff and flail are discussed in chapter 11.

## Ankh
*The color green / life*

The ankh is an all-encompassing symbol of many things. One of the first lessons of the Mysteries is that life-is-all, and the ankh is a symbol of the omnipotence of life.

Water is considered a deep and primordial symbol of life, and therefore we assign the ankh symbol to our great river—or the Negeb—which often appears dark green.

The symbol of the ankh is the key or the knot of life. It may be given, and it may be taken away. It is a direct gift from the Sun God energy.

## Quail Chick
*The color blue*

The newly hatched quail chick is accompanied by two halves of an eggshell and indicates the color blue, because newly born quail chicks have blue feathers.

The eggshells refer to *new, birth, alive,* or *awakened.*

## Flowering Reed-bed on the Nile at First Light
*The color light purple or indigo*

When observed in certain light and at certain times of the day, the flowering reed is distinctly purple. A bed of these fluffy reed flowers blowing in the early morning breeze of first light creates a vivid blanket of indigo.

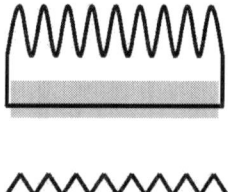

## Hadeda Ibis Feather
*The color dark purple or violet / truth*

The ibis is the most sacred of birds to the Mysteries. The dark colors of the hadeda ibis are alive with vibrant color when observed closely or in the reflection of sunlight. Greens, blues, and purples shine off the glossy feathers, but deep purple is the overriding color and the color associated with highest spirituality. Violet is the color of the seventh (crown) chakra.

Feathers in general mean *truth* within the high-alphabet, but the truth feather that appears below (see Kneeling Initiate) is more common when *truth* specifically is being referred to.

## Water

*Flow / motion / in-motion*

The water glyph seldom appears independently and is usually part of a glyph grouping.

## Energy Rod

*Measurement / is measured/indicated by*

The energy rod is a tool used to measure or manipulate the flow of energy within a person, place, or thing. Therefore, it is also known as a measurement stick/tool or a dowsing/divining wand.

## Worshipping Arms

*Gratitude / worship / humility*

A pair of human arms are uplifted in prayer.

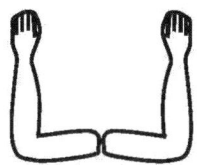

## Brick Wall

*Divine order / structure / cosmic intelligence*

The brick wall or other construction is usually depicted with another glyph, such as the sundisc. The appearance of the brick wall in glyph groupings indicates universal structure within a concept. For example, in the Peace ovoculum (chapter 15), it is cosmic intelligence that gives divine order/structure to chaos in the universal system.

The points on top of the block can be broader, and the glyph may look more like a castle turret in certain images.

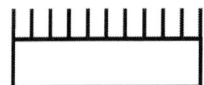

## Kneeling Initiate

*Homage / divine service to life and truth*

The initiate is kneeling. At the initiate's knee is the ankh, the symbol of life, and at the initiate's crown is the feather of truth. These two tokens may be reversed or replaced by the Isis symbol (chapter 8) or sundisc showing the initiate's commitment to love and all-that-is.

## The Feather of Truth
*Truth / universal truth*

This usually appears within a glyph grouping, such as above, although the truth feather can also appear independently. The feather may be patterned with the tricolor primary colors—blue, green, and red—like the snake's ventricles (chapter 16).

The feather is one of Thoth's tools for recording universal truth in Akasha. Where it appears, truth exists.

## The Wasp
*Work / working in or towards*

Wasps work collectively towards a common end; their symbol is the image of hard work and dedication to a synergistic cause. The wasp appears in combination with other glyphs, such as with the hibiscus flower and two eggshells. Examples of these glyph groupings are provided in chapter 16.

## The Goose

*Pair / twin / together / bonded with*

Egyptian geese mate for life and are never apart; hence the symbolism for this glyph. The goose often appears in combination with another glyph, such as the sundisc.

## Quartz Drill

*A building tool used for amplification and communication*

The quartz drill is a building tool whose drill bit is constituted of quartz, which displays remarkable properties. Quartz crystals do not override the natural structures and vibrations of other, harder materials. Instead they seek to match the vibration of these other materials and use the amplified joint-frequency (or sound) to cut, slice, and sculpt the material.

Quartz drills serve a secondary purpose as communication tools, because they are able to emit high and unusual frequencies of sound. These sounds can only be interpreted by trained communicators who decode the frequencies from a distance, rather like those who translate your modern-day Morse code.

If the quartz drill appears along with another glyph, such as the sundisc, it may refer to the sound of the cosmic. Accompanied by water, the quartz drill refers to the flow or transmission of sound waves.

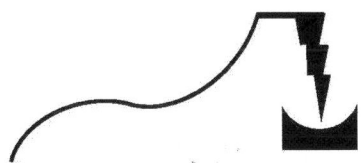

## Priest/Priestess on the Life Throne
*Spiritual leader/teacher*

The priest/priestess sits enthroned as a sacred keeper of divine spirituality within the physically manifested form of a human being. The staff of Anubis represents the delegated universal power that the priest/priestess may use in his or her role as spiritual leader and teacher. (See Anubis, chapter 12.) The Life Throne is discussed below.

When this glyph is used in a horizontal image or ovoculum, the priest/priestess can appear as a kneeling initiate and be separated from the Anubis staff. The meaning, however, is not altered.

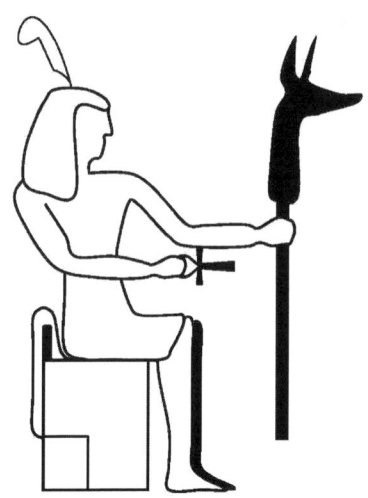

## The Life Throne

*Human journey / divine elevation*

The Life Throne used in the glyph above has its own particular meaning. This is a closer view of the Life Throne.

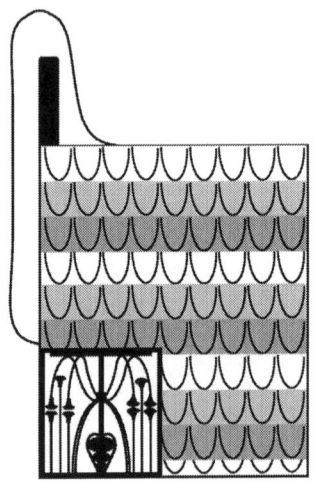

This image is a metaphor of the human journey. A throne indicates that within physical manifestation the human being exists in a state of divine elevation in which he or she contains the potential of the spiritual universe. Human life is a gift through which divine, omnipotent universal consciousness and love may be expressed.

The heart is the energy-center through which this divine universal love may be expressed; it is able to transcend the often inharmonious dual nature of the human being and resonate with the perfect harmony of cosmic peace. Through the heart, balance may be attained in life; it is the platform from which human beings conduct their divine work within living manifestation. The small block within the throne holds the image of the heart-center. The human heart (at the bottom center of the block) gives rise to a platform of balance that contains the left/right split of the papyrus and the lotus or lily. The papyrus plant is representative of material (lower) life on Earth since it tends to hang downwards towards the ground. The lotus is representative of spiritual (upper) life since its flower always points to the heavens. Together, these plants celebrate the dual nature of the human being—both physical and spiritual. (See the Lotus in chapter 16.)

The rhythmic pumping of the human heart mirrors this duality by the contraction and relaxation of the muscles. The heart-center is also the fourth chakra of the human body and so is the central chakra, or point, in the physical body between which the other six energy centers, or chakras, are balanced.

The dualistic papyrus and lotus plants are metaphors of the human circulatory system, since all blood is pumped through the heart and so all cells of the body have a continual opportunity to be energized with pure love-energy. Also, the papyrus is associated with masculinity and the lotus with femininity; the heart-center block in the Life Throne is a continual reminder of the human ability to achieve harmony in duality within physical life.

The heart image itself may also contain the six chambers of wisdom, as explained in chapter 12 under Memnon, and discussed further under the Cobra in chapter 16. Sometimes, two figures may be seen pulling at ropes of a knot that joins the left/right papyrus and lily. This is symbolic of the continual pull that human beings experience on Earth as dualistic creatures.

The full throne is typically decorated with the alternating primary colors of blue, red, and green, whose significance is explained in chapter 7. Bird feathers are also drawn on the throne to show that, like the winged Isis (or the falcon or vulture), human beings are always free to soar to the heights of the heavens; physical manifestation does not condemn the soul to stagnancy. (See chapters 12 and 16 for Isis, the falcon, and the vulture.)

A throne may be considered a seat of power; in human life, this power rests in the heart. The Life Throne describes how Heaven and Earth are united in the human heart and duality overcome.

# 15
## Ovocula of the High-Alphabet

The ovocula (singular: ovoculum) of the feeling- or high-alphabet are seven sacred concepts that receive honor within the school system (see chapters 5 and 14). Although they do not correspond directly with the 7:7:7 vibration and the seven energetic levels, as described in chapter 8, the ovocula are intimately connected to, and reflect, the Seven Rays overall.

# LOVE

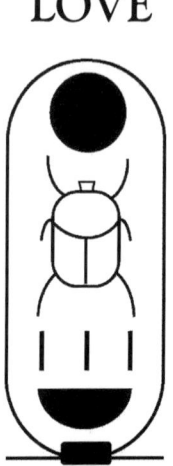

The glyph grouping is contained within an ovoculum since this symbol for Love is one of the seven concepts that receive highest honor and are most sacred.

The ovoculum contains three separate hieroglyphs that are arranged as follows:

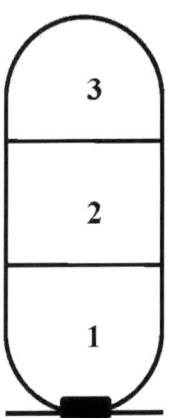

The glyphs may also be arranged horizontally.

Individual glyphs and approximate translations within the context of the glyph grouping:

1. **Half-circle inverted with Three Rods:** These two individual glyphs are interpreted together. Combined, they mean *carrier-of* or *home to* or *gives a place to live or manifest* within the third-dimensional reality of physical space or *living manifestation*.
2. **Scarab Beetle:** The light-bringer, light-bearer, or light-carrier.
3. **Sun:** The Source, source-energy, all-that-is.

**Description:** The scarab beetle or bringer of the light holds the sun in its embrace at the same time that it is firmly rooted in the third-dimensional reality of physical life.

**Interpretation:** The scarab brings life through light, and life is a process of love in evolution. Expressing or facilitating the emotion of love is the method by which divine energy is manifested in life.

**Context/Comment:** The Love glyph grouping is one of the two pillars of wisdom, the other being Light.

**Egyptian equivalent expression:** Omaha. This is a sacred vowel sound.

(Also see chapter 14: Feeling- or High-alphabet Glyphs for a description of these glyphs.)

# LIGHT

The glyph grouping is contained within an ovoculum since this symbol for Light is one of the seven concepts that receive highest honor and are most sacred.

The ovoculum contains seven separate hieroglyphs that are arranged as follows:

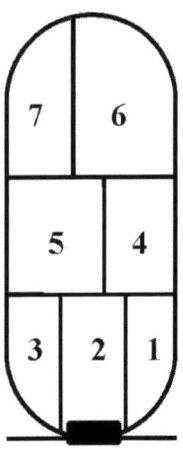

```
The glyphs may also be reversed or arranged
                   horizontally.
```

Individual glyphs and approximate translations within the context of the glyph grouping:

1. **Hibiscus Flower:** The color red.
2. **Flower of the Bulrush:** The color orange.
3. **Golden Staff:** The color yellow.
4. **Ankh:** The color green.
5. **Newly-hatched Quail Chick:** The color blue.
6. **Flowering Reed-bed on the Nile at First Light:** The color light purple or indigo.

    The water and the reed bed in the glyph are often far apart to show that together they make up glyph 6, and should be read on the same line as glyph 7. In other words, the top and bottom of glyph 6 must align with the top and bottom of glyph 7.

7. **Hadeda Ibis Feather:** The color dark purple or violet.

**Description:** All colors of the physical light spectrum are represented.

**Interpretation:** The glyph grouping for Light is a reminder that human beings are manifested energy rainbows in life and therefore contain all the possible light of the cosmos.

The Light ovoculum means much more than visible light within the physical reality. This ovoculum depicts divine/cosmic spiritual light or heavenly rays.

**Context/Comment:** The Light glyph grouping is one of the two pillars of wisdom, the other being Love.

**Egyptian equivalent expression:** Amun.

(Also see chapter 14: Feeling- or High-alphabet Glyphs for a description of these glyphs.)

# TRUTH

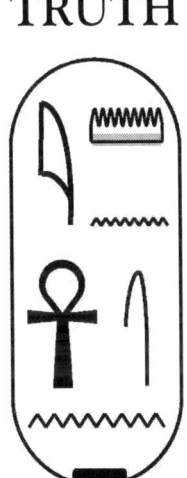

The glyph grouping is contained within an ovoculum since this symbol for Truth is one of the seven concepts that receive highest honor and are most sacred.

The ovoculum contains three separate hieroglyphs that are arranged as follows:

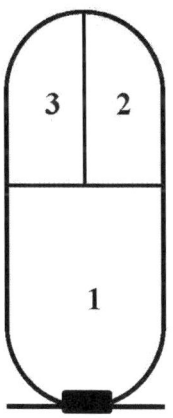

**The glyphs may also be reversed or arranged horizontally.**

Individual glyphs and approximate translations within the context of the glyph grouping:

1. **Water flowing beneath the Energy Rod and the Ankh:** These three individual glyphs are interpreted together. Combined, they mean the flow of life is measured.
2. **Flowering Reed-bed on the Nile at First Light:** the color purple/indigo or illuminated spiritual light.
3. **Hadeda Ibis Feather:** The color dark purple/violet or illuminated spiritual light.

   The water and the reed bed in the second glyph are often far apart to show that they together make up glyph 2, and they should be read on the same line as glyph 3. In other words, the top and bottom of glyph 2 must align with the top and bottom of glyph 3.

**Description:** Truth is a fundamental requirement for the flow of life (uninterrupted evolution), and this is measured by the presence of spiritual light or divine luminescence.

**Interpretation:** Illuminated spiritual light resonates at the highest frequencies of the light spectrum—within the purple/white color band. For illumination (light) to exist, love must simultaneously have been achieved. For love and light to have been achieved, truth must exist, because truth is the basis of love and light. Therefore, the existence of truth is measured by the presence of light.

**Context/Comment:** The Truth glyph grouping is considered the foundation for the two pillars of wisdom: Love and Light. Often, these three ovocula are represented together.

**Egyptian equivalent expression:** Maat.

(Also see chapter 14: Feeling- or High-alphabet Glyphs for a description of these glyphs.)

## PRAYER

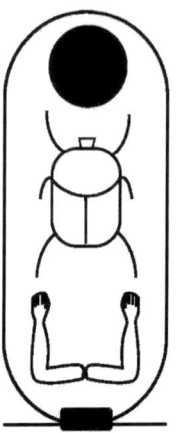

The glyph grouping is contained within an ovoculum since this symbol for Prayer is one of the seven concepts that receive highest honor and are most sacred.

The ovoculum contains three separate hieroglyphs that are arranged as follows:

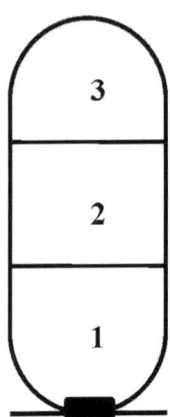

The glyphs may also be arranged horizontally.

Individual glyphs and approximate translations within the context of the glyph grouping:

1. **Worshipping Arms:** A pair of human arms are uplifted in gratitude, worship, prayer, and humility.
2. **Scarab Beetle:** the light-bringer / light-bearer / light-carrier.
3. **Sun:** The Source / source-energy / all-that-is.

**Description:** Humanity's worship of the divine source of light and life is facilitated through prayer.

**Interpretation:** This ovoculum can also broadly be interpreted as worship, surrender, humility, hope, or gratitude. There is no exact interpretation into modern language of the meaning of the ovoculum we are describing here as Prayer. This ovoculum is really a combination of all of these meanings and most aptly applies to the relinquishment of the ego to divine order.

**Context/Comment:** The word *prayer* within the context of this ovoculum does not have the same meaning as your modern understanding of "prayer" or "to pray". Within your societies, *prayer* refers to temporary communication or conversation with the god-energy. Within our schools, prayer means the active participation of rejoicing in the god-energy through the constant and dedicated practice of humility, worship, and everlasting communion with, and belief in, the divine.

The Prayer ovoculum is closely related to the Faith ovoculum since they both describe ideal ways of facilitating divine energy through spiritual practices.

**Egyptian equivalent expression:** Roha-ha or Ro-Ha. This is a sacred vowel sound. (*Ro* is a combination of the vowel sounds *Ra* and *Oh*.)

(Also see chapter 14: Feeling- or High-alphabet Glyphs for a description of these glyphs.)

# PEACE

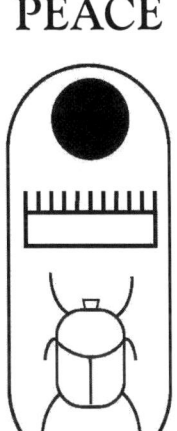

The glyph grouping is contained within an ovoculum since this symbol for Peace is one of the seven concepts that receive highest honor and are most sacred.

The ovoculum contains two separate hieroglyphs that are arranged as follows:

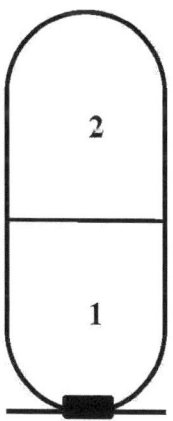

```
The glyphs may also be arranged horizontally.
```

**Individual glyphs and approximate translations within the context of the glyph grouping:**

1. **Scarab Beetle:** The light-bringer, light-bearer, light-carrier.
2. **Brick Wall under the Sundisc:** These two individual glyphs are interpreted together. Combined, they mean the facilitation or support of divine order/structure and cosmic intelligence from the Source.

**Description:** The scarab beetle or bringer of the light carries the divine structure or cosmic intelligence of universal origins.

**Interpretation:** The facilitation of divine order and cosmic intelligence, as was present at the beginning, is the equivalent of the manifestation of peace—it is peace.

**Context/Comment:** The Peace glyph grouping is considered the epitome of what humanity is working towards and the ultimate goal of evolution. Peace is supported by the pillars of Love and Light, which in turn rest on the foundation of Truth.

**Egyptian equivalent expression:** Amen or Fagahr.

(Also see chapter 14: Feeling- or High-alphabet Glyphs for a description of these glyphs.)

# FAITH

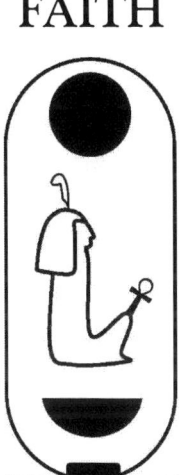

The glyph grouping is contained within an ovoculum since this symbol for Faith is one of the seven concepts that receive highest honor and are most sacred.

The ovoculum contains two separate hieroglyphs that are arranged as follows:

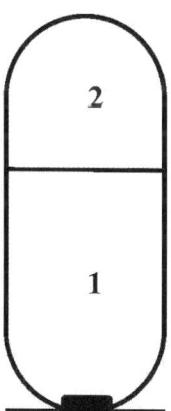

**The glyphs may also be reversed or arranged horizontally.**

Individual glyphs and approximate translations within the context of the glyph grouping:

> 1. **Initiate Kneeling above Bowl:** : These two individual glyphs are interpreted together. The kneeling figure is actively in service to life through spiritual devotion and dedication to the truth. The ankh at the knees represents the individual's service to life and the feather of truth extends from the crown. The bowl means *to serve*.
> 2. **Sun/Sundisc:** The Source / source-energy / all-that-is.

**Description:** The devoted student of spirituality faithfully serves all-that-is through a commitment to truth and life.

**Interpretation:** This ovoculum can also broadly be interpreted as study, learn, devote, discipline, or commit. There is not an exact interpretation into modern language of the meaning of the ovoculum we are describing here as Faith. This ovoculum is really a combination of all of these meanings and most aptly applies to the devoted student of spiritual life.

**Context/Comment:** The Faith ovoculum is closely related to the Prayer ovoculum since they both describe ideal ways of facilitating divine energy through spiritual practices.

**Egyptian equivalent expression:** Oraha. This is a sacred vowel sound.

(Also see chapter 14: Feeling- or High-alphabet Glyphs for a description of these glyphs.)

## SOUND

The glyph grouping is contained within an ovoculum since this symbol for Sound is one of the seven concepts that receive highest honor and are most sacred.

The ovoculum contains three separate hieroglyphs that are arranged as follows:

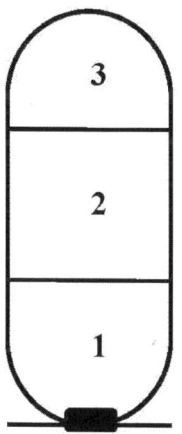

```
The glyphs may also be reversed or arranged
                    horizontally.
```

Individual glyphs and approximate translations within the context of the glyph grouping:

1. **Water with Quartz Drill and the Sun:** These three individual glyphs are interpreted together. Combined, they refer to the transmission of the sound of the cosmic. The quartz drill is used in this instance as a communication tool.
2. **Priest/Priestess on the Life Throne with Anubis Staff:** The embodiment of high spirituality and cosmic power within physical life.
3. **The Sundisc:** The Source / source-energy / all-that-is.

**Description:** The transmission of the sound of the cosmic is the ultimate embodiment of source-energy in our spiritual universe.

**Interpretation:** Sound is a form of manifested energy that transcends three-dimensional life. Sound can convey more than any language or other mental faculty because it speaks directly to our spiritual (or energetic) bodies. Sacred sounds are the method that the universal soul chooses to communicate with all life-forms.

**Context/Comment:** The Sound glyph grouping is the seventh sacred concept of the ovocula series, and it is considered the most all-encompassing of the sacred glyph groupings. This is because there is a sound, or a series of sounds, for every other ovoculum. This is explained in chapter 8.

**Egyptian equivalent expression:** Rama. This is a sacred vowel sound.

(Also see chapter 14: Feeling- or High-alphabet Glyphs for a description of these glyphs.)

# 16

## Glyph Combinations and Animation Symbols

Below are listed some examples of glyph combinations. In your modern day these may be known as sentences, in which more than one concept is conjoined to form a more elaborative meaning. The individual meanings of the glyphs are explored in chapter 14.

We have also included some examples of animation symbols that represent spiritual concepts of the school system. Animation symbols are metaphorical representations of broader sacred universal concepts.

All the images within this chapter are part of the high-alphabet. You will notice that many of the animation symbols and glyph combinations have similar meanings. Within the Mystical Schools we tend to reemphasize the same concepts over and over again, particularly those concepts that revolve around the seven sacred ovocula (see chapter 15). The differences in meaning between the following glyphs are slight and subtle but important.

These are some examples of glyph combinations:

**Example:** *living/alive in the service of love*

The bowl, meaning *service* is underscored by two horizontal lines extending the meaning to *in service to*. The three small dashes below the horizontal lines are symbols of manifestation or *in life*. Underneath the glyph grouping is the Love ovoculum.

**Example:** *openly receptive to working in light*

The wasp means working. The hibiscus flower refers to an openly conscious state. The open eggshells below the wasp and hibiscus reinforce the concept of openness. Below the glyph grouping is the Light ovoculum.

**Example:** *eternal faith*

The goose in hieroglyph means *bonded with*; along with the sundisc, it can mean *eternally bonded to*. When appearing above the Faith ovoculum, the group generally means *in eternal combination with faith* or *eternally faithful*.

**Example:** *life everlasting* or *everlasting life*

The eternal triangle with the ankh means *eternal life as a spiritually conscious being*. As explained in chapter 14, the ankh is a sign of life. The eternal triangle reaches up to heaven, and in its center burns a flame like a candle that reflects the eternal nature of the cosmic soul.

The position of the triangle and the ankh may be reversed.

# Glyph Combinations and Animation Symbols

**Example:** *unconditional love / omnipotent love / all-pervasive love / all-encompassing love*

The Love ovoculum (chapter 15) is preceded by the sundisc combined with the eye patterns of Horus. The eye patterns are part of the All-Seeing Eye that appears later in this chapter.

**These are some examples of animation symbols:**

**Example:** The sun encapsulated by the moon means the balancing of divine male and female energies.

Similarly, cow or goat horns encircling or supporting the sundisc represents the balance of masculinity and femininity.

**Example:** The relief means *in everlasting service to life and truth*.

The ankh alternates with the ankhanet; these are often entwined. A series of bowls supports the alternating pattern. The ankh means *life*; and the ankhanet means *life in motion* and *service to truth*, as well as *spiritual transformation* (see chapter 11); the bowl means *service*. The repeating pattern means *everlasting* or *continuous*.


### The Eye of Horus / The All-Seeing Eye / The Eye of Osiris

The All-Seeing Eye is the animation symbol of Osiris and also, less formally, an animation symbol for Horus (see chapter 12).

The defined eye is ever-seeking truth, like the eyes of kohl (see chapter 1). The tear down the middle of the eye emulates the tear of Horus, the falcon, which is another animation symbol for this glyph concept (see chapter 12, meaning of Horus). The curling proboscis below the eye means *everlasting*; it also represents acute sensitivity to cosmic unfoldment (spiritual evolution). The Eye of Horus is as assertive as it is delicate in its search for eternal illumination.

Through the Eye of Osiris, our internal world is reflected in our external world. The All-Seeing Eye acts as a portal that bridges the essence of who we are as individuals with the totality of all-that-is (represented by the Aten or sundisc). The All-Seeing Eye is able to penetrate our souls and reveal truth of the highest order. If we are living in accordance with the highest good of all, then we have nothing to hide and are in active service to life through the way of Osiris.

## The Lotus Flower

The lotus flower is a symbol of enlightenment, awakening, illumination; and the spiritual or upper life.

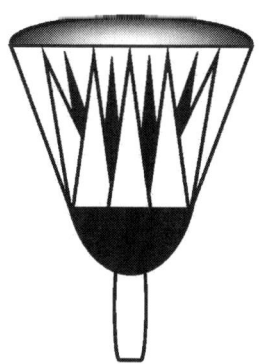

The lotus flower only opens to the sun; the path of the initiate towards illumination may be likened to the growth and opening of the lotus. This is explained fully in chapter 13. Also, the Life Throne in chapter 14 describes the lotus analogy within the context of physical human life, duality, and the heart-connection.

Nephthys (see chapter 12) often accompanies the Light ovoculum and is also closely associated with the lotus flower, which is the animation symbol of spiritual illumination or opening.

Conversely, the papyrus is the symbol of the lower or earthly life (see chapter 14).

**The Boreal Symbol**

The boreal is a symbol of everlasting spiritual life and is usually carried by the vulture or falcon.

On a mundane level, this is the individual's astral body (*ba*), but more inclusively the symbol represents everlasting life through the spiritual body—that which is held in the eternal. Since the spiritual energy is a single source to which all souls eventually return, the boreal symbol reminds initiates that although they are separate in a physical body, their spiritual bodies are forever connected to the divine; all souls form a single, unified entity.

The rounded boreal imitates the eternity of the circle, and the knotted horizontal line below represents the infiniteness of potential life and manifested forms. This is similar to the concept of the ovoculcum, chapter 14. Overall, the boreal symbol means *infinite life through an omnipresent* (but single) *soul manifestation.*

Since the vulture is the father of the sky that holds and protects the soul-energy, the boreal symbol is often seen in the claws of the vulture. Similarly, the falcon carries the astral body away from the physical body during trans-meditation (see chapter 9) and is often seen in glyph transporting the boreal. The snake, as a servant of the creative Sun God energy, can also carry the boreal.

The ring of light at the north pole of the planet Earth—the aurora borealis—reminds humanity of the potential of the boreal symbol. The ring exists upon any astral body whose electromagnetic field is intercepted by solar winds. These are not just those winds of the Earth's sun but of all suns and particularly the Great Central Sun. (See chapter 12, introduction).

## The Cobra

The snake, usually depicted as a cobra, is a servant of the Sun God and reminds human beings of their unlimited creative power to manifest the will of god through their heart-centers. The snake is a symbol of the lower, or earthly, life of physical manifestation.

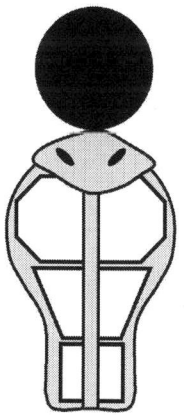

The snake is usually shown with three pairs of ventricles that are symbolic of the human heart. This is explained further in chapter 12, Memnon or Snake god.

When the snake appears crowned with the sundisc, the overall symbol is known as the Uraeus; this symbol re-emphasizes the power of the Aten in the snake's presence. The relevance of the sundisc is explained in chapters 12 and 14. The snake may be winged, which then takes on the additional meaning of the vulture (see below and chapter 12).

A similar symbol to the one above is the snake encapsulating the sundisc, which assumes the same meaning.

## The Vulture / The Vulture's Wings

The vulture is the father of the sky and lord of the upper, or spiritual, world. He reminds human beings of their unlimited spiritual potential, both within the earthly manifested life and beyond. The vulture represents the all-encompassing universe—he is father of the heavens, carrier of astral bodies, and protector of souls. In the vulture's claws may appear two boreal symbols—as he holds the universal soul in his embrace (see Boreal in this section).

The wings of the vulture show human beings that they are able to transcend the limits of their physical bodies and soar with the Angels. There are no limits to spiritual attainment. The vulture's wings echo Isis' promise of life, love, and freedom. See chapter 12, Nekhabet and Isis.

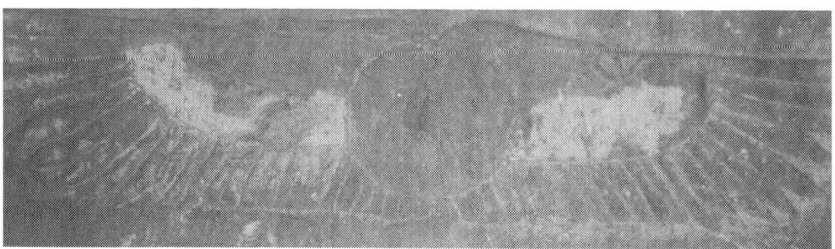

Wherever the wings of the vulture appear, the same meaning is applied. In this image on a temple, the wings extend from the sundisc.

### The Falcon

The falcon, which we sometimes refer to as the hawk, is the animation symbol for Horus and is also symbolic of Ra-Harakhty, as explained in chapter 12.

The falcon assists humanity in gaining great spiritual heights and clarity. During trans-meditation (chapter 9), the falcon facilitates the movement of the astral body (ba) into the ethereal plane; and so the falcon is often seen carrying the boreal symbol in each claw. (See Boreal earlier in this chapter.)

Also see the Eye of Horus in this chapter. The tear of the falcon appears in both images—representative of the spiritual insight or vision of this overall energy.

### The Annual Baboon Calendar

We have a number of methods to mark off time.

The lunar phases and cycles are shown by the presence of the baboon. One baboon equals one lunar month—therefore if seven baboons are depicted, it represents seven months.

The baboon shows how time may be granted or taken away; it reminds initiates of the sacredness of the passing of phases in their earthly lives. In this way, the baboon teaches divine timing and patience.

In our land, our daily lives are regulated by the movement

of the waters of the Negeb. It brings us life and takes life away. In order that societies flourish, it is necessary that we adhere to particular activities within particular months. The initiates of the Mysterie Schools began these work traditions a long time ago, and through the schools the work calendar is respectfully upheld.

The annual baboon calendar is a series of twelve baboons for the twelve months of the year. Next to each baboon appear the glyphs that describe the work activities of that particular month. For example, in Aries (April) when our zodiacal calendar begins, it is spring and a time of low water. The activities for this month are usually building and maintenance, accounting for export, and preparation for harvest. In Virgo (September) the Negeb is at its highest, and during this time of flooding the baboon glyph appears blank—it is a holiday period for us because not much can be done.

Below is an example from the month of Capricorn (January), which is a time of receding water and winter. Our primary activities usually include planting of grains, agricultural accounting, and wine-making.

## The Isis Animation Symbol in Chorus

See chapter 8 for the full intonation series.

The Isis animation symbol is a xylophone of the sacred sounds of Love—the musical scales g, f, and d. Below is the symbol repeated three times showing the overall intonation for the concept of Love.

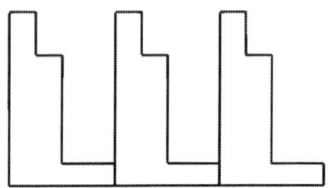

## Nephthys Animation Symbol

The animation symbol for Nephthys is explained in chapters 8 and 12.

The symbol is a singing bowl positioned on a resonator box, which is closely associated with the concept of Light.

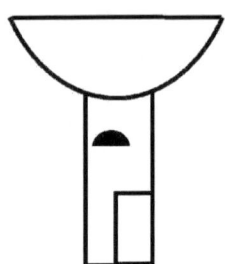

*Glyph Combinations and Animation Symbols* 213

Light and Love are concepts that often appear together; the Isis and Nephthys animation symbols combined are shown below.

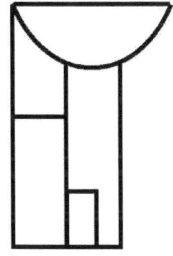

# Epilogue

Thank you for taking this journey with us through aspects of the Pharonic Mystical Schools. We trust that your consciousness has been expanded by truths that have been hidden for a long time.

Wherever you are on the pyramid of illumination at this time is the perfect place for you. As you start to question your level of enlightenment, you will naturally begin to move higher on the illumination spiral and towards the pyramid apex. Energy flows where awareness goes. You may be there already. If so, congratulations!

As spiritual masters of various intergalactic civilizations, we experience great joy in watching the evolution of humanity. From our perspective, the ascension of the human energy system is like an immense spiral of blue/white light, which is gaining momentum every day. We believe that your planet has passed the point of no return. In other words, whatever actions and decisions are made by humanity at large into the future will ultimately pull your group consciousness into ever-increasing spirals of awareness, closer towards planetary illumination. You cannot go back to the darkness that you are currently moving out of—as a child cannot grow back into a baby. However, we also see that you have a long way to go before peace reigns supreme on Earth and amongst all human beings.

# Epilogue

Our role as priests and priestesses of the Mysterie Schools was primarily one that facilitated the illumination of individuals, though with the greater view of influencing overall human spiritual evolution in support of everlasting peace on Earth. Because our schools were destroyed, some may say that we have failed. However, the true test of the Mysteries is invisible to the uninitiated. The very fact that this text has been written, and that it is being read, is all the evidence we need that the Mysterie Schools were not only a success in their time but remain so to this day. Our initiates still walk among you, tirelessly guiding others towards the light, as they were shown the way so long ago. In their roles on Earth, the students of the Mysteries continue to ascend towards illumination, towards Level 7 and beyond to infinity.

As we have explained, the schools were designed to emulate life—not to remove anything from it or to replace it. So even without the school system, those who have chosen the path of self-discovery and inner mastery may achieve illumination independently through life on Earth. We commend those who have taken the difficult and often solitary journey towards enlightenment. Only those who reach the top of their pyramid can know why the journey towards mastery is so difficult but so important. If we do not know who we are, we do not know god and will remain ever separate from our creative source. Once we have discovered god—through ourselves—we are forever joined to all-that-is and eternally alive as spiritual beings.

To live is to love; to love is to know that there is no beginning and no end to life. There *is* no book of life, no manual of illumination, no absolute guide to the mysteries and wonders of this universe that we all share. Life *is* the book of life; as we each grow towards our own highest potential, this concept of life unfolds into a creation beyond our imaginings—it evolves. To participate in this creation is a miracle and the ultimate blessing bestowed to us by god, or source-energy. The great initiations of life are those we put ourselves through, and the lessons we seek to achieve soul growth are entirely of our own making—these are the gifts we give to ourselves.

So please take this knowledge with you into life, and know that you are never alone. The human journey is part of a far greater omniscient spiritual journey, in which all life is simply a series of initiations into a higher and higher way of being.

Omaha, Amun, Maat, Roha-ha, Amen, Oraha, Rama.

# Glossary of Terms

*The terms used for Egyptian gods are described in chapter 12.*

**Akasha /Akashic Complex / Akashic Temple:** A spiritual complex of our universe that exists on a non-physical plane. Akasha is best known for its *House of Records,* in which the soul records of all universal beings are kept, as well as universal information in general. Akasha facilitates many aspects of worship; it attracts beings from all dimensions and galaxies.

**All-that-is:** The Source of creation or source-energy; god/god-energy; the divine; the cosmos; the Aten of our universe (amongst other names).

**Auratic Colombine:** The color-energy channel of the chakra system of the human body. The source of the aura.

**Ba:** Astral body of the human being. See trans-meditation.

**Casket:** See Sarcophagus.

**Chakra(s):** Sacred energy centers of the human body. Seven main chakras extend in a straight line from the base of the body to the crown of the head. The seven centers have a color corresponding to the seven colors of the rainbow, as well as a sound frequency that corresponds to this color.

**Crypt:** The alcoves reserved for trans-meditation. The initiates' sarcophagi are placed inside these spaces, which are usually within pyramidal-shaped mountains or structures.

**Djed / Djed-column / Djed-pillar:** The internal metaphysical structure of human beings, in which peace may reside, and through which a permanent connection to the divine is facilitated. The Djed is likened to a four-tiered tower in which the physical, mental, emotional, and spiritual aspects operate harmoniously.

**(The) Great Central Sun:** A universal sun emitting cosmic light; home to the Sun Gods.

**(The) Hathors:** A highly evolved intergalactic civilization responsible for the original teachings of the Mysteries during the golden age of Egypt.

**High-alphabet/Feeling-alphabet:** The universal alphabet of sacred glyphs and glyph groupings reserved for use within the Mysteries. This alphabet is more conceptual than literal. (The common, or literary, alphabet is the one used for everyday business and communication throughout our land.)

**High-priests/High-priestesses:** Evolved graduates of the Mysteries who move beyond the confines of the school system but who continue to follow a devoted spiritual path. See Priests/Priestesses.

**Higher-self:** The divine, eternal consciousness of an individual that remains in spiritual form but which ideally should guide all activities of the individual within physical life.

## Glossary of Terms

**Initiate:** An individual enrolled in the Mysterie Schools. Also called a student.

**Iyrgr:** The land of Egypt, which means *New Earth*. Pronounced Ee-yar-Gar(th).

**Mana / Per-mana:** A highly evolved state of consciousness enjoyed by the high-priests and high-priestesses. This state is also known as shapeshifting and is recognized by the Sacred Ibis Staff or ankhanet.

**Mysterie / Mystery / Mystical Schools:** A structured system of spiritual learning for initiates who desire the soul's growth toward healing and spiritual illumination or enlightenment. The spiritual teachings and healing practices of the schools are referred to as the Mysteries.

**(The) Negeb:** The River Nile.

**Nevana:** Ultimate illumination / self-mastery / the top of the pyramid / enlightenment.

**Ovoculum:** The oval circlet that contains glyphs of the high-alphabet and appears on stone structures and temples. The plural is ovocula.

**Phara(s):** An initiate who has attained a particular level of mastery—one who has successfully completed all the lessons of the Mysterie Schools up to Level 5 and has achieved Ra-Harakhty.

**Phara-roh(s)/Pharaoh(s):** The pharaohs are students who have completed the seven levels of the Mysterie Schools successfully. Pharaohs are *teachers of the light*, who may teach as priests/priestesses if they desire. Also see Priests/Priestesses.

**Priests/Priestesses:** Teachers in the Mysterie Schools, also known as phara-rohs or pharaohs.

**Ra-Harakhty / Ra-Horakhty:** State of balance between *ka*, *ra*, *ptah*, and *phah* (the Four Teachers of Life). The animation symbol for Ra-Harakhty is Horus the falcon/hawk.

**(The) Ramasseum:** The sound chambers at Abu Simbel, which means *place of the still sounding waters*.

**Sarcophagus / Sarcophagi:** The trans-meditation boxes of the initiates, also known as caskets.

**Sedjaters:** Seekers in our dialect—or students of the Mysteries.

**Sedjes:** Reflectors, specifically cosmic energies reflected at sacred places on the Earth. Sedjes are part of our sodarlory or sacred geometry.

**(The) Seven Rays:** The manifestation of the seven universal chakras (energy-centers). The Seven Rays, also known as the Seven Harmonics, are seven three-dimensional levels of energy with a corresponding color and sound. They combine in synergy to form the Golden Ray—or god-consciousness.

**Sodarlory:** Sacred Geometry.

**Student:** See Initiate.

**Trans-meditation:** The practice of allowing the astral body (ba) to journey beyond the physical realm to acquire mystical information for life on Earth. Also known as transcendental meditation.

**Tomb:** See Crypt.

**Vibrational Chiseling:** The use of sound harmonization to do mechanical work, such as for stonemasonry. Vibrational chiseling is related to the use of sound for lifting and moving objects as well as for healing the human body.

Made in the USA
Charleston, SC
13 August 2015